# *Burma:*
# *The Next*
# *Killing Fields?*

Alan Clements

*With a foreword by*
*The Dalai Lama*

D1564462

ODONIAN PRESS
BERKELEY, CALIFORNIA

Additional copies of this book and others in the Real Story series are available for $5 + $2 shipping per *order* (not per book) from Odonian Press, Box 7776, Berkeley CA 94707. Please write for information on quantity discounts, or call us at 510 524 3143. Distribution to book stores and wholesalers is through Publishers Group West, Box 8843, Emeryville CA 94662, 510 658 3453 (toll-free: 800 788 3123).

*Main editor: Jeff Greenwald*      *Managing editor: Sandy Niemann*

*Research and editing: Leslie McKim, Sally Knight*

*Final editing, inside design, page layout, captions: Arthur Naiman*

*Production coordinator: Karen Faria*

*Notes: Sally Knight, Sandy Niemann*

*Index: Sylvia Coates, Arthur Naiman, Karen Faria*

*Printing: Michelle Selby, Jim Puzey / Consolidated Printers, Berkeley, California*

*Series editor: Arthur Naiman*      *Cover photo: Brian Linklater*

*Series coordinator: Susan McCallister*

Odonian Press gets its name from Ursula Le Guin's wonderful novel *The Dispossessed* (though we have no connection with Ms. Le Guin or any of her publishers). The last story in her collection *The Wind's Twelve Quarters* also features the Odonians.

*Odonian Press donates at least 10% (last year it was 36%) of its aftertax income to organizations working for social justice.*

Clements, Alan, 1951-
    Burma : the next killing fields? / Alan Clements.
       p.   cm. — (The Real story series)
    Includes bibliographical references and index.
    ISBN 1-878825-21-6 (pbk.) : $5.00
    1. Burma—Politics and government—1988-  2. Political atrocities-
-Burma. I. Title. II. Series.
DS530.4.C54 1992
959.105—dc20                                   92-20240
                                                        CIP

Printed in the United States of America      Second printing, October 1992

*This book is dedicated to*
*the thousands of Burmese who have been*
*imprisoned, tortured or executed*
*because they've dared to speak the truth*

*and to*
*Daw Aung San Suu Kyi,*
*winner of the Nobel Peace Prize for 1991,*
*as she continues her courageous*
*"Revolution of the Spirit."*

# Contents

Foreword by the Dalai Lama ................... 4

Acknowledgments ..................................... 6

Maps ......................................................... 8

1/ Terror in the Golden Land ................ 10

2/ The next killing fields? ..................... 21

3/ In Rangoon, city of fear ................... 39

4/ Death and life in Manerplaw ........... 53

5/ Return to the jungle .......................... 71

Epilogue .................................................. 83

How you can help .................................. 86

Recommended reading ......................... 88

Notes ....................................................... 89

Index ....................................................... 92

# *Foreword*

Recent changes in Eastern Europe and the former Soviet Union have provided ample grounds for optimism. Our century has seen a contest between force and regimentation on the one hand, and pluralism, individual rights and democracy on the other. The results of this great conflict are now clear. While no system of government can be perfect, democracy is closest to humanity's essential nature.

In contrast, events in Burma have been cause for great sorrow. Plainly, the greatest source of violence in our world is the existence of large military establishments. The very presence of a powerful military force in a country risks destroying the happiness of its people.

In their elections and the demonstrations that followed, the Burmese people simply expressed their human need for freedom, truth and democracy. The shocking subsequent and continuing brutal suppression of these simple aspirations will ultimately prove counterproductive. Those who practice deception and the use of force may gain considerable success in the short term, but eventually they will be overthrown.

In the past, oppressed people have always resorted to violence in their struggle to be free. In Burma, following in the footsteps of Gandhi and Martin Luther King, Daw Aung San Suu Kyi has led a peaceful and nonviolent campaign for democracy. The practice of nonviolence requires determination, which Suu Kyi and her supporters have shown in full measure.

4

By its nature, nonviolent protest also depends on patience. In this regard, I pray that those who are struggling for democracy in Burma, despite the brutality of their suppression and the struggle they have before them, always remain peaceful.

Their success will depend on strong international support. Signs of late that this is already having some effect should encourage further efforts in the United Nations and similar bodies to influence Burma's military rulers. In rallying such support, increasing awareness is crucial. To this end, the work of the Burma Project USA and the publication of Alan Clements' book *Burma: The Next Killing Fields?,* are most valuable.

I offer my prayers that conflict, killing and oppression will cease and that genuine peace will come to prevail throughout the troubled regions of Southeast Asia.

*The Dalai Lama*

# *Acknowledgments*

Prior to Daw Aung San Suu Kyi's arrest, she described courage as "grace under pressure, grace renewed repeatedly in the face of harsh, unremitting pressure." It is with deep gratitude that I acknowledge my numerous friends within Burma who, at the risk of their lives, repeatedly demonstrated this noble quality while describing to me the truth about their country's crisis.

Among my American friends, I extend my deepest gratitude to the Burma Project's assistant director, Leslie McKim, for believing so profoundly in Burma's struggle for freedom. Her many hours of research made this book possible, and her dedication to bringing this crisis to light is a great expression of compassionate activism.

Another significant force behind the final stages of this book was the Burma Project's administrative assistant, Sally Knight, who selflessly dedicated six weeks of full-time work to typing, editing, writing and researching the manuscript.

I'm also grateful to my publisher, Arthur Naiman; to Christine Carswell, who got the project started; and especially to editors Jeff Greenwald and Sandy Niemann, who consistently inspired the project through its many phases and provided the writing tutelage necessary to make this book a reality.

I'd also like to acknowledge Jack Rendler, Doug Jenks and Jeff Falt of Amnesty International, and Bilal Raschid, Executive Director of American Friends of Democracy in Burma, for providing the basis of the *How You Can Help* section at the end of the book.

In addition, I thank my friends Deborah Anthony, Sharon LaCoix, Julia Zarudzka, Tom Kimball, Louise Lamontagne, Jerry Rosser, Marcia Jacobs, Mitch Davidowitz, Geraldine Devas, Sue Cliff and Bob Chartoff, who supported me throughout this project. And I'd like to thank Susan Garland, who so generously encouraged my last trip to Burma, along with a number of other friends who rallied the assistance needed to make the journey possible.

I'm also honored to acknowledge Catherine Ingram, for initially inspiring me to write this book, and for 25 years of unbroken friendship.

*Daw Aung San Suu Kyi, winner of the 1991 Nobel Peace Prize*

Eureka Cartography, Berkeley

*Burma is almost the size of Texas and has a population of about 42 million (by way of comparison, the population of Texas is about 17 million). Burma lies between 10° and 28° north of the equator, in Southeast Asia, and borders Thailand, Laos, China, India and Bangladesh. Like India, it was a British colony until the late 1940s.*

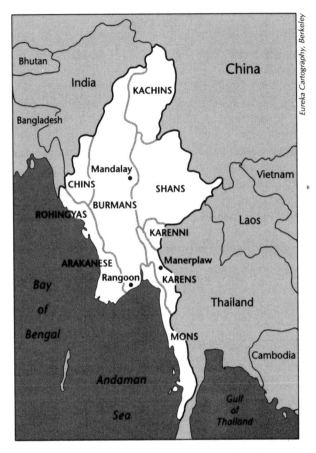

*Eureka Cartography, Berkeley*

*Slightly more than two-thirds of Burma's people are Burmans, the dominant ethnic group; around 9% are Shans and 7% Karens. About 85% of the population is Buddhist. Rangoon, the capital and largest city, has close to three million inhabitants; Mandalay has about half a million. Manerplaw is the jungle headquarters of the democratic forces.*

## Chapter One

# *Terror in the Golden Land*

*I'm lying, naked and cold, on a concrete floor. My back is a landscape of bruises. When I try to draw a deep breath, a piercing agony shoots through my chest, and I realize that my ribs are broken. Struggling to lift my head, I make out the walls of a dim and narrow brick room.*

*My eyes squint into focus and I can see, just in front of my face, a row of thick metal bars rising from the floor. Suddenly reality grips me by the throat. This is Insein Prison, Rangoon—the darkest hellhole in Burma.*

*From a nearby room, I hear dull groans—followed by the snap of thick leather cracking across flesh. A scream pierces the darkness, and the whip cracks again and again.*

*I hear the sound of steps approaching my own cell. "Thu-beh ma lay?" a man's voice demands in Burmese: "Where is he?" I clench my jaw. With a hoarse metallic creak, my cell door swings open, and black leather boots appear before my face. A dark figure leans down over me. He whispers, "Now it's your turn."*

I leapt out of bed, throwing the sweat-soaked sheet to the floor. The summer night was silent, except for the pounding of blood in my ears. For a moment I was lost, trapped in the void between fantasy and reality. Then I heard the distant song of a dove, followed by the soft rumble of a passing plane, and remembered who and where I was.

It was mid-August 1988 and I was in my house near San Francisco. I'd awakened from a recurring nightmare—one of numerous terrifying dreams that had haunted me since my Burmese friend Ko's desperate phone call one week earlier.

Ko and I had been Buddhist monks together years ago when I had originally studied in Rangoon, Burma's capital. I had been thrilled to hear his voice—until I heard the unmistakable sound of gunfire in the background.

"What's going on?," I'd shouted into the crackling static.

Though breathless from running, he described the situation. Several days ago, a general strike had paralyzed Rangoon. Massive street demonstrations were spreading rapidly throughout the whole country. Peasants, scholars, businessmen, monks, students, children—everyone, it seemed, had united in a common cause: democracy.

"And then like lightning, army units appeared. They fired right into the crowds, shooting anybody. It was insane. When unarmed demonstrators got on their knees to peacefully resist the rows of soldiers, they were shot dead. The pavement turned red," Ko said, his voice breaking into sobs.

Hundreds, perhaps thousands, of people had been massacred since then, Ko reported. Soldiers had bayonetted children, shot Red Cross workers as they attempted to aid the wounded and opened fire in front of Rangoon General Hospital, killing doctors and nurses.

The gravely injured were left to die in the streets, while countless others were hauled off to Insein prison—for interrogation, beating and torture. In some instances soldiers threw bodies of the dead and injured into trucks and took them to the cemetery, where the living and dead were cremated together.

Rangoon was clearly in a panic. My friend was in fear for his life and pleaded with me to get him out of the country.

That had been a week ago, and I still couldn't rid myself of the terrifying dream images that Ko's call had stirred. I dropped into a chair and shut my eyes, trying to decide whether to bless or curse the fate which had first drawn me to the distant land of Burma, 10,000 miles from my home.


As a prelaw student at the University of Virginia in the early 1970s, I experienced insecurity, fear, anger, loneliness and a deep sense of mortality. I saw a planet in flames—the Vietnam War, widespread hunger, pollution, torture, pain and suffering everywhere.

I felt I had played out what the world had to offer and that any resolution I might find had to come from within. The teachings of the Buddha, which I had studied some during the previous four years, appeared to be the only source of sanity in an otherwise insane world. So I decided to visit Asia.

When I first arrived in Burma in March 1977, I felt as if I'd come home. The elegance of the people, their generosity and grace, and their extraordinary devotion to Buddhism moved me deeply. I had no desire to leave, but at that time only seven-day visas were available.

Two years later, it became possible to obtain a "pilgrim's visa," provided one had made prior arrangements to study Buddhism in a monastery. In 1979, I was ordained by Mahasi Sayadaw, an elderly Burmese monk and renowned meditation master who was visiting New York. The day after my ordination, I flew to Burma, where I lived for much of the next eight years.

As a Buddhist monk, I plunged into the austere world of traditional monasticism. Following the rules of discipline I shaved my head, took no food after noon and became celibate. Our daily schedule was to wake at 3 am and retire at 11 pm. The days were spent primarily in silence, cultivating the ancient Buddhist practice of mindful self-inquiry, a practice aimed at developing insight into the essential nature of one's own mind.

The experience of life as a monk soon began to sparkle with beauty for me. Everything I needed— food, shelter, health care and a traditional robe— was provided with love and kindness. The teachings were shared in the same way.

After some years of living and studying in the monastery, a dignified man in his fifties was ordained as a monk and moved into the room next to mine. He turned out to be U Tin Oo, a former Burmese Army General and Defense Minister. (*U* is a title of respect for men.)

Burma's dictator, General Ne Win, had been terrified that Tin Oo might lead a coup and had placed his rival in prison for five years. Upon his release, Tin Oo had renounced politics and sought spiritual refuge in the monastery.

*U Tin Oo*

At one point during our year together as monks, Tin Oo led me to a secluded spot on the monastery grounds. "I am Burmese and you are American," he said. "But the Buddha's teachings go beyond nationality or language. I want to see the people of Burma live in a society built on the highest spiritual values, with human dignity and fairness for all. My belief is that love and compassion must be the guiding principles of our political system. I cherish the dream that, before I die, I'll see this vision come true."

Neither of us suspected that U Tin Oo would one day become a national leader in Burma's quest for democracy. But through his friendship, I realized that our peaceful monastery and the community of monks didn't exist in a vacuum. Beyond the temple walls, Burma was struggling to survive one of the most difficult periods in its history—a history that had begun with centuries of wealth and pride, but now placed the nation on the brink of economic ruin and social collapse.

---

European adventurers who first glimpsed Burma in the fifteenth century recognized the "Golden Land" of legend. They returned with fabulous tales of gem mines, vast forests of precious teak, and plains shimmering with thousands of pagodas. There was abundant agricultural land and many deep-water harbors.

When the Europeans returned to colonize Asia, Burma proved a vulnerable target. Despite its ancient Buddhist tradition, the country was riddled with internal strife. Monarchs hadn't been able to establish a stable bureaucracy or a pattern of succession; a king's death invited chaos in the court and bloodshed among aspiring princes.

Cultural differences also produced friction. Burmans, who made up most of the population, lived in the central river valley. *(Burmans* are an ethnic group, while the word *Burmese* refers to any inhabitant of Burma.)

The surrounding mountains and the southern coasts were inhabited by ethnic minorities like the Karen, Karenni, Shan, Mon, Kachin, Chin and Arakanese, each with their own history, language and culture. (See the map on page 9.) Burmans or Shans usually controlled the throne and often enslaved other minorities for massive projects like warfare, canal construction and pagoda building.

The British capitalized on Burma's instability. It took three wars and over 60 years, but in 1886 they took the last Burmese king into captivity and added Burma to their empire. Burma was managed as a province of India, and much of what was authentically Burmese was eliminated.

The British replaced the traditional government with Indian civil servants trained in British methods and encouraged Indian and Chinese migrants to take over business and trade. This turned a profit for the crown and created a new elite of foreign Asians in most Burmese towns. By World War I, Rangoon was dominated by colonial architecture and alien religious shrines.

The ethnic minorities and Burmans, already on less than ideal terms, were further polarized. The British established a separate administration for the hill people and favored some, especially the Karens, for military and government positions. Many Karens, Kachins and other animistic clans converted to Christianity, further dividing them from the Buddhist majority.

By the 1920s, however, students, intellectuals and monks—influenced by leftist ideas emanating from India and Britain—began to organize. In 1935, a young man named Aung San emerged as a potential leader of Burma's struggle for national independence. A law student at Rangoon University, he became a member of the executive committee of the politically vigorous Students' Union, and editor of its magazine. Spearheading student strikes and consolidating alliances, he increased his cadre of friends—and enemies.

In a boldly defiant gesture, Aung San and his closest friends gave themselves the title *thakin*, a

Burmese word meaning "master" which was normally reserved for addressing the British. Calling themselves *thakins* underscored their conviction that Burma belonged to them, not to the occupying power.

*Aung San and his wife at their wedding, 1942*

When World War II erupted, Aung San saw the conflict as an opportunity to throw off the British yoke. After negotiating with the Japanese, he was ready to believe that Burma's salvation lay with them. In 1940, he and a group of like-minded young men known as the Thirty Comrades, traveled to Japan for military training. They formed the core of the Burmese Independent Army (BIA) and fought with the Japanese during their invasion of Burma in 1942.

It quickly became clear, however, that the Japanese had no intention of helping to create a free and independent Burma. They had used Aung San and his comrades as pawns. Realizing this, the BIA switched its allegiance to the Allied forces. Fighting with the British, they defeated the Japanese and expelled them from Burma in 1945.

After the war, the British agreed to grant Burma independence. An election was held in 1947 and Aung San's party won 248 of 255 seats and formed an interim government. The 32-year-old statesman traveled back and forth to London and all over Burma, meeting with ethnic minority leaders and pressing for national unity.

On July 19th, 1947, Aung San was meeting with his party's ministers and colleagues in the conference chamber of a government building in Rangoon. Suddenly the doors burst open; uniformed men carrying submachine guns leaped into the room and opened fire. Within seconds, Burma's new leaders lay dead.

The man responsible for this crime—a political rival of Aung San's—was seized the same day and hanged the next year. Another member of Aung San's party, U Nu, took over. At last, at 4:20 in the morning on January 4, 1948—an hour and date deemed most favorable by an astrologer—Burma became an independent nation, with its own constitution.

But the honeymoon was brief, for Burma was continually embroiled in civil war. Karen, communist and other insurgent groups fought the new government from the hills; the Karens, Shans and Kachins never supported the constitution, believing it underrepresented their interests.

In 1958, U Nu was forced to relinquish power to a junta headed by General Ne Win, who had been one of Aung San's fellow thakins. He was born Shu Maung, but changed his name to Ne Win (pronounced *nay-WIN*, it means "the Sun of Glory").

Burma's constitution permitted minority states to secede after ten years, but Ne Win removed this possibility by "restoring law and order" with his Caretaker Government. He permitted U Nu to be re-elected prime minister in 1960, but seized power again in March 1962.

Superstitious and xenophobic, ruthless and maniacal, Ne Win assumed dictatorial control of Burma, beginning almost three decades of one of the most brutal and repressive governments in the world.

---

My friend Ko had telephoned me during the most massive demonstrations in 26 years of military dictatorship. Unable to ignore his pleas, I dedicated myself to arranging Ko's emigration from Burma. In the spring of 1989, I succeeded.

Even with Ko's safety assured, I could not forget the horrors that my other Burmese friends were facing on a daily basis. As my understanding of the crisis deepened, I was forced to confront an undeniable truth. Burma was not, could never be, just another country to me. Burma was my spiritual home. It was impossible to watch its death throes from a distance.

In November 1990, the overseas edition of *Time* magazine published a cover story which focussed upon atrocities committed against hundreds of Burmese monks who supported the democracy movement. Troops had invaded monasteries, arresting, imprisoning and torturing the monks and nuns.

As accounts of these and other outrages mounted, something deep inside of me shifted. I knew that some of my closest friends were in mortal danger. Even though I was midway through an Australian lecture tour on Buddhist psychology, my priorities became clear. I would return to Burma at once. I was uncertain how I could help, but I needed to be there and witness, with my own eyes, what was happening to the country I loved.

## Chapter Two

# *The next killing fields?*

It was 7 o'clock in the morning on December 4th, 1990. I sat slumped in the back seat of a taxi, hot and exhausted, having just arrived in Bangkok on the overnight flight from Sydney. I told the driver to take me straight to the Burmese Embassy, a decaying, two-story house within minutes of the most opulent hotels in Thailand.

The embassy building had been the scene of random bombings and recent protests by University students and Thai monks. There were iron bars on every window and armed guards kept a watchful eye on one's every move.

I told an embassy official that I had called twice from Sydney, just a few days before, and was here to apply for a short-term tourist visa. I'd been told that such a visa could be granted, if I had the necessary papers.

"No," the official stated. "Impossible."

"But your visa officer told me it was a simple procedure. He said you were allowing foreigners back into the country," I said politely.

"Leave," he responded, pointing at the door. The armed guard looked at me, unblinking, and I understood that the situation was non-negotiable.

Well, at least I'd learned one thing—Burma was no longer the hospitable place I remembered. Even the embassy in Bangkok, hundreds of miles from Rangoon, reflected the fear that had descended upon the Land of 10,000 Pagodas. I could only imagine what life was like within the country itself. Nevertheless, I desperately wanted to return. There had to be a way.

From a hotel near the embassy, I called an underground Burmese contact. His name had been given to me by a dissident Burmese expatriate at one of my lectures in Australia, only days earlier. At the time, I'd thought little of it. Now, my entire journey depended on this sketchy connection. I was enormously relieved when he picked up the phone and agreed to help me.

Late that night, my contact and I stopped our car in front of a large walled residence on the outskirts of the city. My escort rang the buzzer, whispered his name and pushed the door open.

Lying on mats on the pavement of the compound, illuminated by bars of light filtering in through the windows, were the bodies of half a dozen young men. I caught glimpses of their faces; all seemed fatigued and sickly. "These students all have malaria," said my escort as we walked slowly past them. "They've just come in from the jungle."

We found the man I wished to see in a brightly lit interior room. To my astonishment—and his as well—we knew each other. He was an older man; we'd shared a circle of close friends years ago in Rangoon. Showing me a place to sit, he asked what had brought me to this house. I explained what had happened at the Burmese Embassy and told him of my interest of returning to Rangoon.

"I know your love of our country and the family-like ties you have with your Buddhist friends," he said, smiling cautiously. "But Burma's become a land of horror. It's a real risk to enter the country right now. Even if I could get you a visa, it might get you no further than Rangoon airport; after you arrive, they may not let you enter the country. The airport is the junta's chokehold on Burma; they control everything that enters or leaves. But if you still want to risk it, I think we can manage to get you a visa."

Five days later, I picked up my visa from a white-haired old Burmese man at an office near the center of Bangkok. As I turned to leave, the man reached out and held my arm. He reminded me that Burma was still in the viselike grip of SLORC, the junta's State Law and Order Restoration Council. To the Burmese, this sinister acronym represented what SS had to the Jews. "Remember," the man said, "there's only one law in Burma today—SLORC law. It's a synonym for terror and torture. Be careful!"

---

The flight from Bangkok to Rangoon is only 350 miles, but it's a passage between worlds. I'd left the cosmopolitan, highly industrialized "Los Angeles of the East" and within 45 minutes would arrive in what was fast becoming the most impoverished country in Asia. I stared out the window at the lapis curve of the Andaman Sea, and thought about the bitter origins of Burma's present crisis.

When Ne Win took over in 1962, he abolished the constitution and courts, banning all political parties save his own, the newly formed Burmese Socialist Program Party (BSPP). Under the BSPP, all farms and businesses were nationalized. Civil service jobs were taken over by military personnel and profits from private industry were siphoned into the hands of the ruling junta.

Ne Win also attempted to isolate Burma from foreign influences and investment. His severe economic "reforms" and trade restrictions had a devastating effect on Burma's immigrant community, forcing nearly a quarter million Indians and Pakistanis to leave the country without their assets.

Western journalists were soon barred from Burma and replaced by state-controlled media. Tourists were restricted to 24-hour visas (extended to seven days in the 1970s) and confined to a small portion of the country. The Burmese were forbidden to travel to insurgent areas within their own land, and outspoken critics of the regime were imprisoned.

The results were disastrous. By the late 1980s, due to unfettered greed and gross mismanagement of the economy, the Golden Land had become one of the poorest nations in the world. Its once affluent rice industry could no longer meet even local demand, and the government had no means of purchasing foreign-made medicines.

Runaway inflation, coupled with shortages of basic necessities, led to widespread hunger and disease. In 1987, faced with a staggering foreign debt, Burma was forced to apply for Least Developed Country status under the United Nations.

In the midst of this national tragedy—acting on the advice of his numerologist—Ne Win declared that banknotes of 25, 35 and 75 *kyats* were to be abolished without compensation, and replaced by denominations of 45 and 90, the dictator's lucky numbers. It was an attempt to control inflation and profiteering by smugglers, but its most dramatic impact was the immediate destruction of many citizens' life savings.

By early 1988, the Burmese were desperate. Students began organizing demonstrations, demanding the resignation of the BSPP government, a new economic system, full democracy and guaranteed human rights.

Ne Win responded by closing down the universities for several months. But in July, after demonstrations had again picked up steam, he convened an emergency BSPP congress and announced his resignation as party chairman.

The Burmese were not deceived. They knew that Ne Win would manipulate his successor from behind the scenes. Students continued their protests. On August 8, they engineered a huge strike and demonstration that ended in a bloodbath and placed usually obscure Burma in headlines around the world.

According to ABC's *Nightline*, "authorities [later] announced that 500 people had been killed. Foreign diplomats and others on the scene said the number was closer to 10,000." My friend Ko had telephoned me from the center of that storm.

But the movement for democracy had not ended with the massacre. Protestors called for a second nationwide strike on August 22nd. Workers refused to return to their jobs until a new, interim government had been formed. Incredibly, in late

August, the government's brutal repression began to subside. A cautious optimism flowered. Could it be that the tactic was working? Were the military leaders relenting at last?

Organizers who'd been underground surfaced and removed the handkerchiefs that had concealed their faces. Independent newspapers seemed to spring up everywhere. Throughout the country, people resigned their membership in the BSPP.

On September 18, as the strike was about to enter its second month, radio programming was interrupted to announce another "coup." Burma, a male voice reported, was now under the control of the State Law and Order Restoration Council (SLORC), headed by General Saw Maung. (SLORC is pronounced as one word—*slork*—in both Burmese and English.) Its stated purpose was to

*Three leaders of SLORC—*
*Saw Maung (left),*
*Khin Nyunt (upper right),*
*Than Shwe (lower right)*

Dominic Faulder/Bureau Bangkok (all three photos)

restore order while the country prepared for "democratic multiparty elections."

SLORC soon spelled out what restoring order would involve. There was to be a curfew from 4 pm to 8 am, restrictions on giving speeches or chanting slogans, a ban on gatherings of five or more people, and searches for weapons hidden in private homes and monasteries. There was also new, intensified surveillance of all potential dissidents. (The organizers who'd bared their faces the week before discovered that the government now had lists and photographs with which to identify the opposition.)

Within 24 hours, army units raided strike centers throughout Burma. Any dissent, any association with those critical of the regime, meant imprisonment, disappearance or death.

Thousands of students who had supported democracy now had no choice but to face SLORC's terror or flee for their lives. Those who fled were often chased by soldiers for weeks through the mountains near the border. Those who were lucky enough to escape the soldiers tried to make a refuge of sorts in the jungle. There they remain, in one of the most malaria-infested parts of the world—aspiring engineers, doctors, poets, musicians and artists, living under constant threat of attack.

Then, in February 1989, when it seemed that things could get no worse, SLORC announced that the promised "free and fair" elections would actually take place in the spring of 1990. It was as if a dam had broken. Three months after the announcement, 234 opposition parties had registered with the SLORC election committee, announcing over 2300 candidates.

Of all the parties, the National League for Democracy (NLD), formed the previous September, gained the widest following. Its objective—to achieve a democratic government—was simple and appealing. But its greatest attraction was one of its founders, Daw Aung San Suu Kyi. (*Daw* is a title of respect for women. The rest of her name is pronounced *awng sahn soo CHEE*, but she's normally referred to in English simply as Suu Kyi—*soo CHEE*.)

Suu Kyi is the daughter of Burma's revered national hero, Aung San, the man who would have been Burma's first prime minister if he hadn't been assassinated in 1947, when Suu Kyi was two, shortly before he was to take office.

*Aung San Suu Kyi (in the foreground) with her mother, brothers and father, Aung San*

In 1960, her mother was appointed Burma's ambassador to India and Suu Kyi, then fifteen, went with her. She went to school in India and then at Oxford.

In 1972, she married an Englishman, Michael Aris, and worked for the United Nations in New York. They lived for several years in Bhutan, where their two sons were raised.

Suu Kyi retained her Burmese citizenship and continued to visit her

*Burma Project USA*

*Suu Kyi at the age of about six*

mother in Rangoon. In early 1988, her mother suffered a severe stroke, and Suu Kyi went back to Burma to care for her.

At first, Suu Kyi watched the demonstrations from her mother's bedside. But after the August 8th uprising, she could no longer keep silent. She wrote to the government, asking it to form a committee to address the protestors' demands. Then, on August 25, she made her first public speech, at the famous Shwedagon pagoda. She told a cheering crowd of several hundred thousand people that "I could not, as my father's daughter, remain indifferent to all that was going on."

The crowds saw her as Burma's last ray of hope for overcoming 26 years of oppression. As she began traveling around Burma for the NLD, she captivated ever-larger audiences with her "Revolution of the Spirit" campaign. She advocated discipline, sacrifice, unity of purpose, multiparty democracy and nonviolent civil disobedience.

If the opportunity for free elections seemed too good to be true, that's because it was—and SLORC's real purpose soon became clear. Rather than force the democratic parties underground, where they might create an effective opposition, SLORC gave them the opportunity to expose themselves. It dangled a carrot, then dealt swiftly and mercilessly with those who took the bait.

SLORC first placed draconian campaign restrictions upon the parties. Public campaigning was already limited because of SLORC's anti-assembly law. But now all speeches, writings and publications had to be preapproved by local township authorities. They confiscated any derogatory material; those found guilty could receive prison terms of up to three years.

The restrictions were a success; only the most outspoken opposition voices and their intimate supporters appeared in public. But Suu Kyi and the NLD refused to be intimidated. They defied laws forbidding public meetings and continued to print political manifestos despite SLORC's orders. Suu Kyi wrote:

The behavior of the Chairman of SLORC is not that of a *gaung saung* [leader], but that of a *gaung shaung* [evader of responsibility]. To resolve problems...we must meet face to face. Why do you [Saw Maung] not have the courage? Why do you still hold the gun?....[If the leaders of SLORC aren't] willing to engage in dialogue, they are not fit to run a government, not fit to administer the nation....Solving enigmas by using lethal weapons on unarmed civilians is a fascist method.

In a letter to her husband in January 1989, Suu Kyi described the oppressive tactics SLORC used against her:

We started our journey...by boat. All the way the people in both villages and towns had been told not to go out of their houses, not to wave...and gunshots had been fired to frighten them. Yesterday we sailed into Bassein accompanied by two boatloads of armed marines, and the whole harbour was full of troops, most of the streets blocked, sandbagged and barbwired, and hundreds of soldiers posted all over the town. Also, they arrested a number of our men.

On another occasion, Suu Kyi was campaigning in the southern delta region. As she walked toward a group of soldiers, a SLORC army captain ordered his soldiers to aim their rifles at her. Suu Kyi asked her followers to move aside and continued down the center of the street. Before the troops opened fire, an army major intervened and ordered them not to shoot.

Whenever she spoke, thousands of citizens gathered, risking imprisonment by defying the anti-assembly laws. Later SLORC arrested, tortured and murdered her most visible supporters. And yet, despite the continued intimidation, Suu Kyi vowed that her people would continue their Gandhian-style civil disobedience campaign.

Young dissidents were asked not to make defamatory statements against the armed forces, for Suu Kyi believed that "there is a difference between the armed forces and those who abuse the power of the armed forces."

Her influence also extended beyond the NLD; she was not only able to check violent confrontations and control her less disciplined supporters, but also to inspire nonviolent approaches in other political groups.

Repressing political campaigns was just one of SLORC's tactics. Soon after announcing the elections, it began another, far more aggressive effort to thwart its opposition: forced relocation. This term refers to moving entire neighborhoods out of Burma's population centers into rural backwaters, where they could not follow or participate in the democratic movement.

Here's how the *New York Times* described the forced relocations:

> At least 500,000 Burmese are being forced to move from cities to new, ill-prepared outlying towns where malaria and hepatitis are rampant. Diplomats described seeing Burmese families sitting along the roadsides by their demolished houses with all their belongings, waiting for up to three weeks for army trucks to take them to relocation sites. The diplomats, who were interviewed by telephone or

in Bangkok, said the relocations have been taking place in most major cities.

*B.U.R.M.A.*—the Burma Rights Movement for Action—reported that in these so-called "new towns," people live in ten-foot square thatched huts, perched over flooded, mosquito-ridden swamps. Families are sometimes forced to sell their clothes in order to buy enough rice to feed themselves every *other* day.

In the midst of the ongoing relocations, Suu Kyi was to lead a huge rally on July 19, 1989, to celebrate Martyrs' Day, a national holiday honoring her father's assassination forty-two years earlier. An estimated 10,000 SLORC troops flooded Rangoon in anticipation of the rally.

According to the *New Yorker,* a government edict had been released the day before, giving SLORC officers the authority to arrest any participants and mete out one of three punishments—three years hard labor, life in prison or execution. Suu Kyi called off the rally. She said her party "had no intention of leading our people straight into a killing field."

The day after Martyrs' Day, SLORC stationed eleven truckloads of armed troops outside Suu Kyi's home in Rangoon. When she tried to leave to pay a private visit to her father's grave, she was placed under house arrest for "endangering the state."

SLORC also arrested her immediate staff and imprisoned almost all other members of the NLD's executive committee. Its 64-year-old chairman,

U Tin Oo—the man I'd come to know during my days as a monk—was sentenced to three years' hard labor. (Seven more years was added to that in February 1992.)

After Suu Kyi was arrested, she "demanded a transfer to Rangoon's Insein Prison and asked to be kept under the same conditions as her supporters who were arrested as part of the crackdown on her party." SLORC ignored her request.

*Suu Kyi at her home in Rangoon in late 1988*

She immediately began a hunger strike that lasted for twelve days, breaking it only when she "receiv[ed] solemn assurances from the authorities that her supporters were not being subjected to inhuman interrogation and that their cases would be dealt with by due process of law."

When the elections finally took place in May 1990, only 93 of the original 234 political parties fielded candidates. In a stunning and humiliating upset for the junta, Suu Kyi's NLD party won 392 of the 485 seats up for election in the National Assembly (81%), while the military only won 10 seats.

But SLORC did not transfer power to the new National Assembly. The obvious reason, of course, was a desire to retain power. But Philippine Foreign Secretary Raul Manglapus, after meeting with SLORC leaders in December 1991, suggested another motive. SLORC leaders, he said, were afraid they'd face "Nuremberg-type trials" if they relinquished control to the opposition.

In the end, the only concrete result of the "free and fair" elections was that there were now as many as 30,000 political prisoners, including many of the winning candidates.

The fate of these prisoners has been described by Amnesty International, which identified nineteen interrogation and detention centers throughout the country. All employ torture on a routine basis. Prisoners are severely beaten with thick leather straps, given electric shocks to the genitals, stuck with needles in their finger tips and burned on sensitive body parts. Some dissidents, including young students no more than fifteen years old, are placed in solitary confinement for up to six months.

Those who have escaped or been released from prison have described other barbaric methods, which are now so institutionalized that the torturers refer to them by name. The "iron road" is when an iron bar is rolled up and down your shins until the skin is rubbed off. "Walking the seashore" is being forced to crawl on broken glass while being beaten and kicked. The "wet submarine" is being submerged naked in a tank of water until nearly suffocated. The "helicopter" is being hung from an electric fan and then spun around and whipped or beaten with a stick. The "ice treatment" is being stripped naked and tied to a large block of ice.

The torture continues until the prisoner gives SLORC the information it wants.

---

"Coffee, sir?"

The singsong voice of the stewardess jolted me out of my grisly reverie. In the distance I could see the Burmese coast; it wouldn't be long now.

As I sipped from the plastic cup, I tried to fit the jagged pieces of information together in my mind. The scenario in Burma seemed somehow familiar. It reminded me of something, and by the time we began our descent toward Rangoon, I'd figured out what.

A few years before, I had attended a dinner party at the home of John Bryson, a well-respected photojournalist who for years had been a *Life* magazine correspondent and photo editor.

Sitting in John's living room, I'd browsed through his portfolio and come upon an old copy of *Life*. The cover photograph drew me in. It showed a group of brutalized Cambodian children, huddled closely together, expressions of horror on their faces.

"What are you looking at?" John had asked, breaking my concentration.

"*Life*'s cover story on the Cambodian genocide. Did you shoot this article?"

"Yes," he said, shaking his head. "My God, what a trip that was. I and a few other journalists were to be the first western press allowed back into Cambodia since its fall, four years before. We knew we'd be in for some gruesome scenes, but what we saw went beyond anything we could have imagined."

Bryson reached for the magazine. "Here, turn the page," he said. "That photo up in the corner is the one that shook me up the most. We walked into a large open field, which was full of human skulls—just like the photograph shows. Not just hundreds, but thousands upon thousands of white, dried skulls.

"To get the shot we walked out through them. When we looked closer, we realized that almost every one of the skulls had been broken, cracked or had huge holes in it. Some still had bandanas over the eye sockets, where the victims had been blindfolded."

"Unbelievable," I said. "It sounds like an absolute nightmare."

"It took a while to fully comprehend what we were seeing. *Each skull represented a human life.* Each had once belonged to a human being with skin, blood, a family—and they all had been bludgeoned, or hacked with huge machetes, or clubbed to death.

"We stopped in the middle of this sea of skulls and just stood there in disbelief. These were the killing fields. And there were many of them, not just one. It was almost impossible to comprehend the reality of it all. We all asked ourselves the same question: *Didn't anyone know?*"

As I recalled that conversation now, an awful question arose in my mind: Would the next killing fields be in Burma? The more I thought about it, the more parallels I saw between the Khmer Rouge in Cambodia and SLORC in Burma.

Pol Pot's Khmer Rouge had systematically destroyed scores of Cambodian villages and launched mass relocation campaigns. The terror was especially aimed at those whose education could be a threat to the regime. City dwellers were driven to the countryside and then purged of "bourgeois elements"—including those who simply wore glasses or spoke a foreign language. Refugees fled Cambodia by the thousands—if they were lucky enough to escape. Pol Pot even changed the name of his country to Kampuchea.

In Burma, SLORC has also destroyed villages and set up relocation camps. Many thousands of Burmese have been intimidated into submission, imprisoned, tortured and executed, and SLORC's fury has been particularly focussed on students and other educated people. Refugees are streaming to the mountainous border regions and into Thailand weekly. Ne Win also changed the name of his country, to Myanmar.

But there's one way in which things have the potential to become much worse in Burma than in Cambodia—it has six times as many people.

## Chapter Three

# *In Rangoon, city of fear*

From the moment I stepped off the plane in Rangoon, it was evident that the character of this beautiful land had changed. On the airport roof, a group of tense SLORC soldiers manned a machine-gun post. I walked across the runway tarmac, preparing my story for the immigration authorities.

Inside the airport terminal, the tension mounted. Our planeload of mostly young Burmese officers and their families, along with an official tour group of five European businessmen, was greeted with silence by several members of Burma's secret police.

Their presence was intimidating: stiff legs placed shoulders' width apart, arms firmly crossed and fists clenched. All wore dark sunglasses. They scrutinized the passengers' every step.

This was my first encounter with SLORC troops— Burma's killing machine. I knew that most of SLORC's 280,000 foot soldiers were poor, simple rural boys, many just teenagers, who desperately needed money for their families. With inflation running nearly 70 percent and the entire economy in shambles, SLORC had little problem recruiting these young men or programming them to believe they were upholding justice.

As our group waited to pass through immigration, an officer broke the silence. "Mr. Alan Clements, come forward," he commanded.

I had been warned this would happen. Although my name appeared on the flight's official passenger list, it didn't tally up with the list of approved arrivals. This was not a moment to panic. Trying to look calm, I walked forward and was escorted by several uniformed officials to a back room of the airport.

Inside the small, smoke-filled room, the SLORC official conducted a grueling, two-hour courtroom-like examination of my motives for re-entering Burma. Having spent many years there as a monk, I stated my desire to revisit sacred sites and monasteries. He eyed me suspiciously, but finally relented—after I paid a sizeable "donation" to be given, he claimed, to a nearby monastery.

"You can stay for two days only. And you're not to leave Rangoon," the cigar-smoking officer concluded, stamping my passport with a snide chuckle.

Relieved but by no means relaxed, I made my way outside. I'd been cautioned in Bangkok, by an underground Burmese official, to "be careful of how they play you at the airport. If authorities have the least bit of suspicion about you, they may pretend to go along with your story—let you in—hoping to kill many birds with one stone. They might gamble that it's to their advantage to allow you entry, then have the police follow you, locate your contacts and grab them after you leave."

Had I been tricked or was I free? One thing was certain—I had now entered a city of fear. Once out of the airport, I was utterly on my own.

With only two days in Rangoon, I hadn't a moment to waste. Leaving the airport, I hired a taxi. "Where you going?" the driver asked, eyeing me in the rearview mirror.

"Downtown." As we drove into the city, I stared reflectively out the open window and remembered the land and people that had touched me more than any other culture in the world.

Rangoon had never looked cleaner. Many roads were newly paved and walls freshly painted. Flowering shrubs had been planted along roadsides. There were more parks and bridges, and many new buildings. But something was off. What was missing was Rangoon's unique ambiance; the sense of entering an extended village or community.

SLORC had launched a "beautification" campaign soon after they'd taken power, trying to demonstrate the benefits of restoring law and order. They'd demanded that all Rangoon's residents paint their homes by the end of the year— or face utility cutoffs. These municipal improvements were a veneer of respectability, I realized, engineered to distract from the suffering that lay just below the surface.

As we drove on, modern Burma's true face revealed itself. At almost every major intersection there were large red-and-white lettered propaganda billboards erected by SLORC. They read, in Burmese and English: *Love and Cherish the Motherland, Only Through Discipline Will Democracy Be Won* and *The Military is Here To Protect the People From All Riotous and Destructive Elements.*

When I reached my hotel I telephoned the US Embassy and told the officer on duty my name, passport number, hotel and flight departure information. I explained that I was most likely under surveillance, and that if I wasn't on my scheduled flight in two days, the embassy should assume the worst and try to find me.

From this point on, I took no chances. Anything I said or did had to be done with impeccable discretion, for fear of endangering those with whom I'd be in contact. SLORC had filled Burma's prisons with thousands of innocent men, women and children on the slightest suspicion of dissent towards its policies.

As I walked around the city that afternoon it was clear that people were avoiding me. Their faces appeared strained and weary as they moved quickly along. Others had their heads lowered, unwilling to meet my eyes. This was so different from my memory of the Burmese people.

Gone were the days when even a casual passerby would stop and ask a western visitor to have tea and talk about international politics or Buddhist thought. Gone were the days when one would be openly invited into a Burmese family's home to have dinner and meet the elders of the household. I felt that I was witnessing the death of the most elegant culture I'd known.

Some time later, taking circuitous back roads to be certain I wasn't followed, I arrived at the compound of an old friend's house. She was a well-known Burmese filmmaker, now nearly 80 years old. Her family had become my adopted relatives during my tenure as a monk, and we rejoiced at seeing each other after so many years apart.

Taking my hand, she led me into a small room near the back of the house. She locked the door behind us and peered out the window, "Secret police are everywhere," she said, closing the blinds. "Every store, every corner—SLORC's evil eyes are everywhere, throughout the whole country. You can't trust anyone anymore. You can't even have an overnight guest in the house, unless you report it to SLORC authorities the same day. They can give you up to seven years in prison."

"Does that just apply to foreign guests?"

She shrugged. "It doesn't matter who. It could be your own brother. Anyway, I'm too old for prison," she said with the wry humor I remembered. She'd always been a feisty woman who'd stood up for her beliefs. "But I'm glad to see you again," she said energetically. "Let's talk."

Among the many stories she shared about living in a "SLORC-induced state of terror," the most compelling was her eyewitness account of a recent murder. "Just a few weeks ago," she said with a slight shudder, "I saw SLORC secret police fire at a group of children who had gathered on a street corner and were chanting anti-SLORC slogans. Out of nowhere, undercover agents appeared. The children started running and screaming as the police pulled out their guns. They shot a ten-year-old boy right in the head. It was horrible. The police just stood there, remorseless and proud, as if they had saved the country."

I could tell that my friend had found it emotionally exhausting to recount these tragedies. But as

I was about to leave, she gripped my hand. "Never before have we experienced a darker period than this," she said bitterly. "Not even during the Japanese barbarities we had to suffer during World War II. It's like waking up to the most unimaginable nightmare, day after day. Sometimes you forget; you see the trees, the flowers. But then you hear screams in the night, and you know that another person has been taken away."

I took a taxi back to my hotel, ate quickly and then telephoned an old friend who'd been a judge during the democratic years in Burma. He was glad to hear from me and agreed to meet at my hotel—but only after dark.

While waiting, I turned on the hotel's television. It provided yet another lesson in SLORC-controlled "Big Brother" politics.

National news consists of short video clips of SLORC events, thinly disguised as legitimate news stories. I'd heard that the clips usually propagated SLORC's self-proclaimed "magnanimous intentions," celebrating the "noble" qualities of General Saw Maung and the head of military intelligence, Major General Khin Nyunt *(kin NYUHNT)*. They were often shown in public dedicating yet another park or flower garden, restoring yet another pagoda, paving yet another city street or bestowing donations on another monastery.

The two generals now appeared on the screen, walking between long lines of carefully placed citizens who bowed to them as they passed by. Some tossed flowers at the generals' feet. All the while the two despots smiled, waved and shook hands with the minions as a soundtrack of ebullient cheering was heard in the background. Looking more closely, however, I noticed that the people in the crowd were neither smiling nor cheering. They appeared stiff and frightened.

There was a knock at the door. I stood up and turned off the television.

"Who is it?," I demanded.

"It's U Gyi," said a quiet Burmese voice. I quickly let him in.

"Uncle!," I said enthusiastically. "It's great to see you! You weren't followed...?"

"That's impossible to know." He settled himself in a chair. His frail shoulders hunched forward and he squinted at me intently through thick glasses. "No place is safe anymore," he said, accepting a cup of tea. "Not even within the monasteries. SLORC has secret police disguised as monks and nuns. There are unseen eyes everywhere.

"No one speaks about politics. Many people have begun to distrust their closest friends." He shrugged and ran a thin hand through his white hair. "After a while, when so many people end up mysteriously disappearing, you gradually shut up. You live in constant fear of accusations from informers—then imprisonment and torture. Fear governs what you say and what you do.

"When people get arrested, who knows where they're taken? They're never heard from again. That's the tactic SLORC is so masterful at using. The more individuals missing, the more terror there is. The more terror, the less unity. And without unity, there's no opposition."

U Gyi leaned back, removed his glasses and rubbed his eyes. "We also feel that SLORC takes a perverse joy in making people suffer. Especially that Khin Nyunt. He's the mastermind behind the cruelty; he's turned torture into an industry.

"This I know for a fact," he said. "My two nephews and my niece—they were students at the university during the '88 uprisings—were all arrested. We still don't know the boys' whereabouts; we think they may be dead." His voice was calm, but his hands shook slightly. "My niece is with us at home. She was repeatedly raped and beaten in prison. She wakes us up, screaming, in the middle of the night."

U Gyi finished his tea and carefully set the cup down. "I must be going now," he said. As we walked toward the door, I knew this might be the last time we'd see each other. He turned away and walked slowly down the long corridor. I stood in the hallway and watched, completely at a loss for words. When he reached the end of the hallway, U Gyi stopped, turned and regarded me with a judicious eye.

"Never mind!," he called out to me. "Be on your way! You've got work to do."

After a restless night, I woke early and decided to visit a small village not far from central Rangoon where I'd often walked as a monk, collecting my alms food each morning. The village held many memories and was the home of numerous friends, both young and old.

Village life centered around a small temple. Since I'd known the caretakers of the temple—an elderly blind man and his wife—quite well, I wanted to see how they had fared over the past years. But as I approached the area I stopped short. The village and temple were gone. In their place was a vacant, bulldozed lot.

I recalled the times I'd walked through this exquisite and ancient village, savoring the early morning smells of my favorite Burmese foods cooking on open coal stoves. Children had prepared for school, villagers clad in colorful sarongs had bathed around the outdoor wells. I was often greeted by small groups of children, kites trailing behind them as they raced down the road.

Their delight was a great source of inspiration for me after the monastic silence and long periods of isolated study. Many of the children I had watched growing up over the years had visited the monastery during their long summer breaks and had been ordained as novice monks. Now they were gone, moved to "new towns" along with thousands of others SLORC had labeled "undesirable." They were probably starving, diseased, maybe even dead.

Other contacts I met that day told similar stories. A recently dismissed university professor, now working as a taxi driver, described SLORC's control of information and the economy as he drove me back to my hotel.

"SLORC is trying to hide what it's doing from the world," he said. "The only news we get is *Voice of America* and the BBC. If you don't have a radio, or if it's a blackout day, you don't know what's happening."

He swerved to avoid an oxcart loaded with water-melons. "If there's an article about Burma in *Time* or *Newsweek*, it's blacked out in the magazine. And what we get from the local, SLORC-controlled papers is worthless—lies and propaganda."

As we entered a back alley near my hotel, my professor-turned-taxi-driver discussed his own fate. SLORC had closed Burma's high schools and colleges after the 1988 uprising, since the students had been the main voice of the prodemocracy movement. Thousands of teachers and professors were fired and forced to join the students as they fled to the malaria-infested jungles along the Thai-Burmese border.

"An entire generation of educated Burmese is being destroyed." The driver shook his head in disgust. "We're no more than animals under this military junta."

After a brief rest back at my hotel I ventured out again. The sun was setting. As I walked up a back road to the Shwedagon pagoda, the gentle sound of temple gongs reverberated in the quiet evening. Looming ahead, the 2300-year-old Buddhist shrine rose 300 feet into a bright orange sky.

The western face of the pagoda's huge golden dome was radiant, reflecting the setting sun. Here, for a moment, I was able to recapture the feeling that had pulled Burma so deeply into my heart.

As I walked up the long staircase to the upper portal of the pagoda, I passed familiar bookstalls containing ancient Buddhist texts and temple bells of every size and shape. Small flower shops exuded the exotic fragrance of jasmine. Everywhere were statues of the Buddha. The Burmese are famous for their artistry, and the gilded sculptures are among the most beautiful one can find anywhere.

I found a shopkeeper I'd known well over the years, and inquired about a monk friend I wanted to meet. Leaving his stall unattended, the merchant led me through lantern-lit alleys until we arrived at an unfamiliar house. Fifteen minutes later my monk friend entered, accompanied by a second monk.

*"Ashin Paya!"* I exclaimed, using the honorific greeting given to revered monks. "I'm happy to see you after all these years." We spoke for a few minutes, after which he introduced his friend, a younger monk named Aloka who had recently been arrested on suspicion of belonging to the All Burma Young Monks' Union (ABYMU). This activist organization had redefined the potential role of the clergy in Burmese society by calling for immediate transfer of power to the democratically elected government.

"I was arrested by the authorities back in October," Aloka began, "during a big SLORC crackdown on monasteries in Mandalay. They took me into detention and began to viciously interrogate me. When I saw a nearby room filled with monks' robes, I feared for my life. Still, I refused to admit I'd done anything wrong.

"Meanwhile, I heard screams from other rooms in the prison—incredible screams, like nothing I'd ever heard before. So many other monks had been arrested that I was sure it was one of my friends.

As I sat there in terror they began slapping me across the face and shouting, 'You're next, if you don't tell us who other members of the ABYMU are!' But I offered them no answers and they beat me with a cane pole against my legs and shins."

He lifted his robe. His legs were so severely bruised they looked like they had been pounded with a baseball bat. "See here," he said. "This is how SLORC supports the religion of our people."

Aloka's injuries, he insisted, were minor compared to what many other monks have faced. He described how hundreds, maybe thousands of monks had been arrested; exact figures are impossible to get.

Most of those brought in were charged with possessing anti-SLORC literature, using heroin, being communists—even raping women. Three young monks were arrested solely for the poems they'd written in their journals.

"Many of the monks were given long prison sentences," Aloka told me. "Others were killed. Still others fled and are now in hiding. A number of the highest-ranking monks have been detained, some of them forcibly disrobed. Many are 'missing' and presumed dead."

The *sanga*, or community of monks, has always been a powerful influence in Burma, where 85% of the population is devoutly Buddhist. Monks are held in the highest esteem; they personify the spiritual aspirations of the people, sacrificing worldly pleasures in favor of strict adherence to the teachings of the Buddha.

So when the *sanga* began supporting the demonstrators, SLORC was hesitant to repress them too harshly. But in August 1990, when the students peacefully demonstrated to commemorate the massacre in Rangoon two years earlier, troops viciously attacked the entire gathering—including thousands of monks who were also attending the event.

After much deliberation, the clergy responded with an unprecedented measure. They decided to boycott the Burmese military and their families. They refused to accept their alms or to administer Buddhist rituals for their weddings or funerals.

The implications of this spiritual banishment are profound to a Buddhist. It eliminates the opportunity to acquire spiritual merit and virtually assures a rebirth in the animal realm, or in hell.

SLORC retaliated by attacking all 133 monasteries in Mandalay, where they tortured, killed and forcibly disrobed many monks.

I asked my host about the program I'd just seen on SLORC-controlled TV, which showed Saw Maung and Khin Nyunt visiting monasteries and making large donations to senior monks.

"Pure SLORC propaganda," the monk replied. "After the raids on monasteries, some high ranking monks were replaced by puppets—monks controlled by SLORC. Sure, SLORC wants people to believe that they support Buddhism. But no one is fooled by such nonsense. SLORC leaders treat dogs better than they treat monks."

I walked back toward my hotel alone, shaken by the day's encounters. The streets were empty; there was a chill in the air. My final night in Rangoon was painfully long. I slept fitfully, anticipating my departure from Burma the next morning.

The taxi drive from my hotel to the airport took me down University Lane, directly past Aung San Suu Kyi's home, where she has languished under house arrest since July 1989. As we drove slowly past the heavily guarded compound I reflected on Suu Kyi's dramatic political rise in Burma.

Everything I'd read and heard about her inspired me: her dignity, her enormous courage, her uncompromising commitment to truth and her skillful integration of the principles of Gandhian nonviolence and political leadership. Her urgent call for reconciliation among the diverse peoples of her country stirred my own passions to join her "Revolution of the Spirit."

"It is not power that corrupts, but fear," Aung San Suu Kyi wrote in her book *Freedom from Fear.* "Fear of losing power corrupts those who wield it, and the fear of the scourge of power corrupts those who are subject to it."

I looked at her silent house, wondering if she would ever be allowed to lead her people into the future.

## Chapter Four

# *Death and life in Manerplaw*

Bangkok is one of the most exciting cities in Asia, a sprawling metropolis that pulses to its own manic rhythms. Outside my hotel the street swarmed with taxis and an all-night market threw its phosphorescent glow against my window shades. The night was hot—every night in Bangkok is hot—and the low throbbing of the hotel's air conditioner filled my room with a long, sustained sigh.

I couldn't sleep. For hours I lay fully dressed upon my bed, completely restless but uninterested in the distractions available just outside my room. My visit to Burma had moved me profoundly; I would never forget the whispered conversations, or the pall of fear and helplessness that lay like smog over the land. I was staggered by the suffering I'd encountered and awed by the fact that so many people had been willing, even eager, to risk their lives by speaking with me.

But my two-day reconnaissance of Rangoon, under the myopic eye of SLORC, had only amplified my desire to understand the real story behind the people's struggle for national independence. Clearly, this could never be accomplished under the conditions imposed during my recent visit.

Frustration gave way to anger; and anger, at last, to an unwavering sense of conviction. I wouldn't leave Southeast Asia until I'd met, face to face, with the democratic forces camped along the Thai-Burmese border.

The next morning, underground dissident students helped me arrange an illegal, two-week visit to northeastern Burma. The route into the rugged mountain areas spanned hundreds of miles and was fraught with danger. We would be entering a war zone where thousands of SLORC's most seasoned guerrillas were attacking democratic forces.

My Burmese student guide, our Thai driver and I sped through the night towards a border town 300 miles northwest of Bangkok. Our final destination was Manerplaw—the remote jungle headquarters of the All Burma Students' Democratic Front (ABSDF), located along the Moei River in an area of Burma under the control of the armed forces of the Karen National Union (KNU).

The ABSDF was born in the jungle in November 1988, after the summer massacres in Rangoon, Mandalay and other cities. Of the original 10,000 high school and university students who'd fled from the cities, fewer than 3,000 remain. These men and women, now living in primitive camps scattered through 700 miles of mountainous terrain, are among the most outspoken enemies of SLORC tyranny. Fighting alongside the Karen soldiers, they help keep the democratic hopes of their nation alive.

The dramatic decrease in the students' ranks had numerous causes. Lacking the natural immunities of the local population, many died of malaria, dysentery, cholera or malnutrition. Others had been captured by SLORC soldiers. Some

*Dr. Naing Aung, MD, chairman of the ABSDF*

had been drafted into service as military porters, a job they held until they died of exhaustion.

Still other students had slipped back into Burma's urban centers, overcome by the extreme hardship of life in the jungle. They were in hiding, not even daring to contact their families. Other escaped dissidents remained concealed within Thailand, where they're considered illegal aliens by the Thai government and are subject to arrest and deportation if caught.

In the past, Thailand had been more charitable. When thousands of Burmese students had begun pouring across the border after the August 1988 massacre, Thai authorities ignored SLORC's demand that they be repatriated and granted them asylum. But after the commander-in-chief of the Thai army, General Chaowalit, visited Rangoon in December 1988, the situation reversed.

Chaowalit set up a repatriation center near the Burmese border and pleaded over radio and television for all Burmese students inside Thailand "to resume their studies and become good citizens." The general repeated SLORC's pledge that the students' safety would be guaranteed. Those who believed the announcement met a disastrous fate, as Amnesty International reported:

> Nine returning students were arrested by soldiers...and taken to a military camp where four of them were allegedly beheaded....In another case...fifteen university students, including three women, were executed after they were captured on their way home from the border areas. The three young women were repeatedly gang-raped before being killed.

As we pressed ahead toward the Burmese border, my 20-year-old guide summarized the aspirations of the Burmese resistance. "People all over Burma want to live freely," he said matter-of-factly. "This was made clear by the elections. We want democracy, for the people and by the people. That means human rights, freedom from brutality, being able to walk, breathe and think without the fear of being taken by soldiers at any time of the day or night."

Later in the journey, I listened intently as he recounted an experience he had during one of the marches.

> At the time of the demonstrations, I was an English major in my last year at Rangoon University. I had my hopes set on moving to the countryside and teaching English to the village children.

When the demonstrations started, I knew that this was our moment. Aung San Suu Kyi inspired us to stand up for our rights and to speak our conscience. Together with most of my classmates, I joined in the demonstrations. Several of my younger brothers and sisters wanted to come out and march too.

He took a deep breath and continued with difficulty.

None of us had any idea what would follow. It was September 1988, just before SLORC seized power. We were marching in the afternoon—hundreds of thousands of us. My 15-year-old sister had her arm through mine. My younger brother, who was 11, was holding her hand.

Up ahead the troops suddenly appeared with their guns pointed at us. We were unarmed and walking peacefully—and then the shooting started. All I heard was screams and gunfire. Hundreds of people in front of me fell to the pavement. My sister and I began to run, until her limp body knocked me over. She had been hit. I watched as she bled to death within a few seconds.

My little brother was in shock at seeing his sister dead. He kept hugging her and wailing. But we hadn't a moment to stop, so I grabbed his hand and ran. Just a few feet later he was shot in the back of the head. I began to scream. I picked his body up in my arms and continued running. I knew he was dead yet I kept running, all the while screaming aloud.

Once in the nearby village, I lay in the dirt beneath the floor of a small hut, my brother's bloodied body on the ground next to me. I was crying desperately, but dared not make a sound. The soldiers ran by along the foot path. Only when it got dark did I dare to leave.

We buried my brother near our home. My sister's body was never found. The next day I left Rangoon and, along with many friends, began the trek into the jungle.

Arriving at a town near the border at 3 AM, we changed to a four-wheel-drive truck. We picked up several other ABSDF members, packed medical supplies, blankets and food provisions, and drove on into the dawn.

As we drew closer to SLORC's front lines, I noticed a gradual change in my perceptions. Perhaps it was only my projected anxiety, but the lush jungle mountains began to lose their enchanting beauty. It was becoming clear, intuitively, that we were entering a war zone.

As we drove, my escort pointed out Burmese villages just across the river that had been burned and destroyed. Sometimes SLORC would conduct a public torturing of local villagers in order to terrify their fellows into submission.

That had happened, he said, in a village called Chaungsone. A monastery there, run by a respected abbot, provided shelter and help to the needy—students, the local Mon and Karen people, even soldiers from the Burmese Army.

One afternoon a group of SLORC soldiers arrived at the monastery. They seized the abbot and began torturing him. The monk was stripped and his body sliced with knives. The soldiers filled the bleeding wounds with salt before tying the naked abbot to a tree. The local people were forced to watch the monk suffering; those who cried or reacted in any way were kicked and beaten by the soldiers.

By now the sun was high. We continued in silence until my Burmese companion abruptly told the driver to stop the truck. He then motioned for me to get out. "I want to show you something; over there," he said, pointing up ahead.

We walked down a narrow path through dense foliage. After a few minutes, we entered a vast open space. "This," my companion said, "is a 'teak barn.' " It was a flat clearing, nearly a square mile in area, filled with thousands of logs.

There are many such "teak barns," most of them owned by Thai military officers under contract with SLORC. They're part of a multimillion dollar lumber and logging operation that clears teak forests deep within Burma, transports the wood to Thailand for milling and sells the products on the international market.

The United Nations Development Programme issued a report in July 1991 which stated the extent of this devastation. Recent satellite photographs show that an area larger than the state of Massachusetts is being cleared each year. As a result, Burma now has the fifth highest deforestation rate on the planet. Since it has virtually no reforestation plans, the country will be denuded within fifteen years. The lush rainforests along the Thai-Burmese border may not last another five.

It's easy to understand why SLORC is trying to crush the democracy movement. But why is it raping Burma's exquisite environment?

When the Burmese military suppressed all dissent in September 1988, the United States suspended aid to the regime. Japan and the European Community followed. The military junta had to find other means of financing its operations, so it began selling off Burma's natural resources—mostly teak, fish, oil and tin.

"The cynicism of the Burmese regime has, regrettably, found ready partners amongst Burma's neighbors," US Senator Daniel Moynihan told Congress.

> A large number of Thai companies...have, with the cooperation of the Thai government, signed concessions to cut millions of tons of logs inside Burma....Firms from other countries, including Hong Kong, Japan, Singapore and Europe, have reportedly participated in the teak concession bonanza in Burma. In addition, at least 15 fishing concessions, worth over $17 million, have gone to Japanese, Thai, Malaysian, Singaporean, Australian and South Korean fishing companies.

> The money from these concessions will not help ordinary Burmese....Rather, the profits will prolong the life of the current government and equip the Burmese military for yet more violence.

Multimillion dollar deals with SLORC oligarchs have also been made by Western oil companies—including Amoco and Unocal in the US, Petro-Canada, and BHP of Australia. US multinational corporations have invested over $125 million in SLORC's economy since 1989 alone.

Actively wooing increased US investment, SLORC hired Van Kloberg Associates, a Washington DC public relations firm, "to improve its image in the United States and hopefully attract lucrative US business investment."

Van Kloberg has a distinguished portfolio. The firm's other clients have included Saddam Hussein, the infamous Liberian military leader Samuel K. Doe and former Romanian dictator Nicolae Ceausescu. Van Kloberg himself was reported as saying that former Ku Klux Klan leader David Duke's defeat in the Louisiana governor's race was "a pity" and that freeing Poland from German control after WWII "should never have happened."

SLORC's profits from legal exports pale in comparison to its earnings from Burma's real cash crop—opium. There's evidence that Burma supplies a *majority* of the heroin sold in the US, and that SLORC has played a major role in doubling Burma's opium production to more than 2200 tons a year.

SLORC has also permitted Burmese drug barons to build heroin refineries, a far more lucrative business than merely harvesting and exporting the product. Bertil Lintner, a political expert on Burma and writer for the *Far Eastern Economic Review*, says he has photographs of SLORC military trucks carrying the chemicals needed to process opium into heroin.

The US *Congressional Record* reports that, in September 1991, Chinese and SLORC troops descended on the border town of Wanting and ordered people to stay in their homes. Shortly thereafter, two convoys of military trucks rumbled into the village—one from China, the other from inside Burma. Soldiers then exchanged loads of Chinese arms for Burmese heroin.

China is actively strengthening its ties with Burma. In September 1990, it agreed to sell SLORC $1.2 *billion* in arms. The shipment included eleven Soviet-made jets, numerous gun boats, about a hundred tanks, dozens of anti-aircraft guns, rocket launchers and assault rifles. Since Burma has no external enemies, the only possible use for such weapons is against the country's own citizenry.

There's also evidence that both police and military officials are profiting from brothel gangs that operate in Burma and Thailand. This isn't as well documented as the heroin trade but, according to UNICEF, at least 40,000 young Burmese women and children have been sold into Thailand's infamous sex industry. The girls are imprisoned within brothels and become the property of their owners. They are often forced to serve up to 20 clients a day and run a high risk of contracting AIDS.

An article in *The Australian*, a national newspaper, described the fate that befell some of these girls in 1991. Thai authorities had rescued 25 Burmese women, aged between 18 and 35, from a brothel in southern Thailand. All were HIV positive. The girls mysteriously "disappeared" once they were repatriated, and it was later reported that they were taken from their homes in Burma and given lethal cyanide injections.

Former Australian Human Rights Commissioner, Justice Einfeld, describes how "the Burmese Government...gave the go-ahead to inject with cyanide *thousands* of female prostitues affected with the HIV virus in the hope of eradicating the disease from the country."

The setting sun was hard in our eyes as we bumped along mountainous dirt tracts. At last we skidded to a stop beside a small log bridge that had collapsed. Below, wedged into the ruins of the bridge, lay a large truck.

Turning around would mean a seven-hour detour, so we decided to hike the final five miles into the jungle. It wasn't a thrilling prospect, but we had no choice. We trekked for hours, following the pale beam of a single flashlight. The jungle creaked and whispered ominously. I heaved a sigh of relief when, utterly exhausted, we heard the Moei River flowing just ahead.

We bathed, ate the cooked rice we had brought along and wrapped ourselves in our clothes to gain what protection we could from the swarms of mosquitoes. I fell asleep under the stars.

At sunrise I was captivated by the beauty of the area. The sky was fiery orange, marbled with pastel blue. A range of jagged, majestic peaks was straddled by clouds. Both banks of the Moei were shrouded in dense, deep rain forest, echoing with the calls of exotic birds. A few hundred yards downriver, a small herd of water buffalo bathed at the river's edge.

Despite appearances, this was no Shangri-la. I had arrived in one of the most war-ravaged regions of the world. At any moment the idyllic dawn could be shattered by a sudden air attack, or the hacking sound of rifle fire.

Although I was worried for my own safety, my visit would be brief, and I had an American passport. Barring a fatal ambush, I'd be back in the US in time for Christmas. The lives of my companions—and the tens of thousands of other refugees in the area—were in much greater danger.

Even now, all three of my companions appeared incredibly weak and were sweating profusely. As we climbed into the riverboat that would take us the final two hours downriver to Manerplaw, two of them began to vomit. Only then did I learn that they, like all of the other students I was to meet in the jungle, had malaria. During many of the nights to come, bunked with dozens of students in makeshift shelters, I was kept awake by their retching groans.

After passing through numerous Karen military checkpoints, we arrived at the headquarters of the ABSDF in Manerplaw. The deplorable living conditions of the exiled students were immediately obvious. Shelters were generally small, open-sided bamboo huts. Blankets were scarce and personal items nonexistent.

Meals consisted mainly of white rice and liquid fish sauce, with an occasional fried egg shared four ways. Medicines were rare, as was suitable drinking water. The river was the only source—and for three months of the year the monsoon churns it into a filthy torrent. In spite of all this, and a recently intercepted transmission revealing SLORC's plans to bomb within the next few days, spirits were high.

The two weeks I spent with these Burmese students—working in the infirmary, sharing simple meals and discussing the hopes for their country—were among the most meaningful of my life. It was particularly inspiring to meet several young men in the camp whom I'd known as monks, years before, in Rangoon. Deciding, at least for the moment, that direct action was more important than silent meditation, they had disrobed and joined the resistance after the uprisings.

One evening I was speaking with a dignified 29-year-old Burmese woman, a university graduate who'd fled her home after the uprisings of 1988. As we sat under the night sky, with a small candle burning between us, we discussed the principle of nonviolence: How can it be effective against an oppressor like SLORC, which tortures and kills unarmed civilians? At what point is self-defense necessary, if only to survive?

In the near distance we could hear soft guitar music and the voices of students singing love songs—a nightly occurrence. Groups of students would gather and walk with guitars, stopping at the huts of resting fellow students. As we listened to the music, I spontaneously asked my companion if she'd ever been in love. She paused for some time and regarded me evenly.

Yes, I have been in love. Two and a half years ago my fiance and I were to have been married. We loved each other very much. We had known each other from childhood.

This was in 1988. But the demonstrations began only two weeks before our wedding. It was an incredible moment in our lives. We so desperately wanted freedom and democracy. The moment had come when we thought it would be possible to come out from under the boot of military oppression that had trampled us since we were young children.

First we went out and marched. The next day my sister and brothers came out with us. The following day my mother and father came out, then my aunts and uncles, until my whole family was in the streets. Suddenly, from nowhere, the soldiers appeared. They grouped together in three long rows with their automatic weapons and bayonets aimed at us.

We in turn, many thousands of us, knelt down in front of the soldiers. We sang to them, "We love you; you are our brothers. All we want is freedom. You are the people's army; come to our side....All we want is democracy."

But they had orders to fire, and they did. Many students, some friends and some of my family members were shot dead on the spot. We had no idea that our own people would kill us. I was terrified. I could scarcely believe it was actually happening. There was blood everywhere and loud screams, and the cracking of gunfire echoed loudly. Everyone panicked and ran for cover. People began falling down everywhere—a young friend of mine died in my arms. I looked for my family. They were gone. My fiance and I began to run.

The soldiers rose from their positions and began to chase us. We ran for shelter, but the soldiers continued to pursue us. There was more firing and more people began to fall as they were shot in the back. Still we went on running. We scattered and ran into the forest and on into an outlying village. But the soldiers were right behind us, so we had to keep on running.

We ran ever deeper into the forest. We couldn't see, stumbling everywhere, cut, scraped and scared. Still we were chased into the night. We huddled together in the trees, frightened that the soldiers would catch us and kill us without mercy.

We went on running for the next two weeks, deeper and deeper into the jungle. I was still with my fiance, along with a dozen other students, and we miraculously managed to evade the soldiers. Sometimes we had to bury ourselves under leaves, cling to the banks of rivers, or stand rigidly behind trees as soldiers passed by.

We felt like animals being hunted, sleeping sporadically on the forest floor. It was cold and unbearably painful. We were constantly bitten by ants and mosquitoes. Yet, we managed to stay alive.

After two weeks of running, nearing exhaustion, we all contracted malaria. We were extremely weak, feverish and nauseated. That night the soldiers ambushed us. It was to have been the day of our marriage—instead, my fiance and I were separated during the firefight.

I have never seen or heard from him since that night. I don't even know if he's alive or not. I dare not contact his family or my family, because it would put them in great danger if SLORC found out. If they're not already dead, that is.

We sat without stirring. The candle flickered in a temporary breeze and time seemed suspended. "I still think about him," she said. "I do miss him sometimes. But being out here in the jungle for these past few years, living under the tyranny, my values have changed. My love is now of a different order. I'm in love with freedom. And even if I'm caught and tortured to death, if it will help restore freedom in my country, I will die in love.

"Yes, I have been in love," she said softly. "And I remain in love."

On December 18, 1990, my last day in the jungle, an important event took place. Dr. Sein Win *(sane WIN)* and eight cabinet members (who were among the few democratic leaders who'd avoided capture and imprisonment by SLORC) risked their lives to make the rugged, five-day journey to Manerplaw. They brought momentous news.

At secret meetings in Mandalay and Rangoon, Burma's elected representatives and leaders of various minority organizations had decided to form a Burmese government-in-exile. Sein Win had been appointed its first prime minister.

After arriving in Manerplaw, Sein Win and his colleagues entered further negotiations with ethnic groups, students and monks, all of whom agreed to unite under a common banner. Such a show of solidarity would, they hoped, help them win recognition from the nations of the world.

In a crude wooden meeting hall crammed with foreign correspondents, Sein Win announced the new National Coalition Government of the Union of Burma. Everyone knew this bold step would have serious repercussions. The formation of a parallel government was SLORC's worst fear, and we all feared they'd turn Burma into a sea of blood before they'd tolerate such a challenge.

During my final night in Manerplaw, I wandered around the isolated camp. Walking barefoot along the moist dirt path, I could see the dim glow of a kerosene lantern from the camp infirmary ahead.

*Meeting in Manerplaw to announce the formation of the National Coalition Government of the Union of Burma (NCGUB). From left to right: Brang Seng, chairman of the Kachin Independence Organization; Dr. Sein Win, prime minister of the NCGUB; and Gen. Bo Mya, supreme commander of the Karen National Union.*

There, in a makeshift medical tent, I met a student suffering from a severe case of malaria.

Despite the cold night air he was sweating, lying nearly unconscious with an IV needle in his arm. He had a fever of 105 and had begun urinating blood.

The young man's friend was standing beside him. "Malaria's not the only thing that's wrong with him." He lifted his friend's blanket—the boy's leg had been blown off. He lifted his shirt—there were bullet wounds in his neck and arm. A raw shrapnel scar, ten inches wide, sliced across his chest.

The boy was fifteen years old; he'd been a ninth grader in Rangoon before fleeing into the jungle

after his brother and sister were killed in the August 8 massacre.

Struggling to speak, he whispered to me, "I hope you have learned how precious freedom is by your visit to the jungle. Please tell your people the truth of my people's situation. We want democracy and we need help. Please. We need it *now.*"

The boy himself was beyond help; he died the next day. Yet as I recall him, lying on a bed of wooden planks, my memory focuses not on his awful wounds but on the blood-stained T-shirt he was wearing when he died. It read, "Our heads are bloodied, but they are held high."

*Fifteen-year-old boy whose leg was blown off by SLORC troops, at an infirmary in Manerplaw. He died the day after this picture was taken. SLORC also killed his brother and sister.*

## *Chapter Five*

# *Return to the jungle*

1991 brought both bad and good news. In August, I learned that the friend who had escorted me to Manerplaw nearly a year ago, along with over 40 other Burmese students, had been captured and imprisoned by Thai immigration police.

While in detention, my friend had been beaten unconscious by the police. He sustained multiple fractures and numerous other injuries to the face, head and body. On finishing his jail term, he was forcibly returned to Burma. There, he and his comrades were no doubt imprisoned, tortured and probably executed by SLORC.

One ray of light did, however, penetrate Burma's continuing darkness. On December 10th, Daw Aung San Suu Kyi was awarded the Nobel Peace Prize. The official statement read, "The Norwegian Nobel committee wishes to honor this woman for her unflagging efforts and to show its support for the many people throughout the world who are striving to attain democracy, human rights and ethnic conciliation by peaceful means."

In February 1992, while preparing the manuscript for this book, I received an unsettling report. Major General Khin Nyunt, appearing on Burmese television, had declared that SLORC was about to launch a major military offensive. Their objective was to overrun Manerplaw and crush the democratic resistance once and for all.

As SLORC troops descended upon Manerplaw, horror stories began flooding out of Burma. In January, 700 Muslim youths died of suffocation after being herded into warehouses. SLORC troops had opened fire inside a mosque, killing 200 Muslims at prayer. Muslim women were being gang-raped and left to bleed to death, while their crying children were thrown on the roadside. Half a million Kachins had their homes and villages destroyed. It seemed that SLORC was preparing for all-out genocide.

The stories were carried by a vast flood of refugees, mostly ethnic minorities. During the first few months of 1992, more than 225,000 Rohingyas (a Muslim group that lives along the western border) fled to Bangladesh. About 10,000 Kachin refugees escaped into China's Yunnan Province. Some 60,000 Karens and Mons had fled the SLORC troops, and thousands more were crossing the border into Thailand weekly. Even in the remote and mountainous region of northwestern Burma, thousands of Naga Hills tribespeople fled into the Indian states of Mizoram and Manipur.

By now I understood the importance of witnessing these events myself. I hastily arranged a flight to Bangkok. After two more days of overnight bus and truck rides, I arrived once again at the banks of the Moei River. Across the turbulent water lay a burning Burma.

The two-hour boat trip, downriver to Manerplaw, was punctuated by the deep and haunting percussion of heavy artillery, mortars and rockets exploding in the distance. Our boatload of tense, heavily armed Karen soldiers crouched low until we arrived at the banks of the besieged democratic headquarters.

Jumping ashore and running up the steep river bank, I entered Manerplaw. It was a ghost town. Except for several high-ranking Karen officials, a few members of Aung San Suu Kyi's democratic party, the government-in-exile's prime minister Dr. Sein Win, and a handful of armed soldiers, Manerplaw was virtually empty—a mere skeleton of what it had been a year before. All able-bodied men, women and sometimes even children as young as 10 years old, had been mobilized to defend the area from the rapidly advancing SLORC troops.

That night the cool mountain air and a blanket of thick fog enveloped the remote settlement. Anxious and unable to sleep, I walked around the grounds seeking familiar faces. Now and then the urgent static of a walkie-talkie pierced the dark; I was startled by the unexpected blast of an exploding rocket echoing within the steep mountainous ridges surrounding us. I knew that my student friends and the Karen soldiers were fighting for their lives just a few miles away.

The next day, unwilling to remain behind the scenes, I got clearance to travel to the front lines. I made the short boat trip down the Moei River under military escort, then navigated down the Salween River amid sporadic mortar fire. The Mae Pah Ridge, rising beyond the hills that surround Manerplaw, loomed 4100 feet above the riverbank.

Along its precipitous slopes lay dense jungle canopy, where thousands of SLORC guerrillas were assaulting the 4,000 Karen and other freedom fighters dug in along the ridge. If the Mae Pah Ridge fell, Manerplaw would be at the mercy of SLORC's heavy artillery.

Suddenly I noticed a bloated and mutilated body floating nearby, face up. The man was naked except for his underwear and a scarf tied around his neck. Both arms, pulled from their shoulder sockets, were bent behind his back. There were large chunks of flesh missing from his inner legs, indicating he'd been tortured. His face was swollen and black, and it appeared he'd been bludgeoned to death with a rifle butt or large stick.

This was the usual fate of military porters, and SLORC had enslaved 20,000 of them during the last three months in this area alone. These porters, usually young men, were forcibly seized and taken into the war zone to serve as pack animals for military supplies and as human mine sweepers. Numerous shallow mass graves were being discovered throughout the region, filled with the mutilated bodies of these conscripted laborers.

By midafternoon I arrived at the small Mae Pah supply camp, which was bunkered into the earth along the swirling green water of the Salween River. Soldiers were dug in deeply to protect themselves from mortar and rocket attacks. A constant stream of casualties was being brought in from the jungle, carried on bamboo-and-burlap stretchers. They were loaded onto river boats and rushed to the makeshift hospital across the river.

One screaming man in bloodstained clothes was carried into camp lying on his stomach. Whole pieces of his back were missing. As the writhing body was carried past, I turned to an onlooker and asked, nearly fainting, "Will he survive?"

"No, he'll be dead in a couple of hours," the man replied matter-of-factly. "Do you know how that man's wounds were caused? They came from the Swedish-made Carl Gustav rocket. It's designed to explode in the air and project razor-sharp pieces of shrapnel over a wide radius. It's the most lethal weapon SLORC has used against us thus far."

"A Swedish-made rocket?" I said in astonishment. "How has SLORC gotten Swedish-made rockets?"

"We think they were obtained illegally through Singapore. We don't know how." He shook his head, walked off and jumped back into his bomb trench. I wondered what Alfred Nobel, the Swede who had established the Peace Prize that Suu Kyi had just won, would think of all this.

A few days later I was allowed to interview a small group of recently escaped Burmese porters. Most of them had been found by Karen soldiers, starving and quivering in shock while wandering aimlessly in the jungle. One of them shuddered visibly as a translator helped him recount their ordeal.

SLORC soldiers came into our village, killing people at random. Others started gang-raping our wives and daughters—especially the younger girls. Hundreds of us tried to flee, but the soldiers had encircled the village. Most of the men—but many women, too—were herded like animals and told that we were now military porters. We could take nothing with us except the clothes on our bodies.

Over the next two months each of us had to carry heavy loads of munitions. I carried four grenade launchers (about 50 lbs.) over the steep mountain tracks. We were regularly beaten with large sticks and rifle butts. With little water and half-cooked rice only once a day, sometimes only every other day, we grew weary and sick. After several weeks I didn't care whether I lived or died.

I watched many of my comrades fall sick. Often SLORC soldiers would just kick our exhausted friends over the ridge or down a steep hill and leave them for dead. Many were beaten in the face with rifle butts until they were nearly unconscious; then the soldiers would cover the victim with leaves and light the leaves on fire. Others were simply shot.

There were maybe 80 women in our group. At night they were forced into a separate area. The SLORC soldiers would take any girl they wanted. Some women were gang-raped up to eight times; we could hear their screams and cries but could do nothing. Sometimes we knew that it was a friends' wife or daughter—or even our own. My wife disappeared somewhere along the way. She could have been one of the many women who bled to death after being gang-raped.

Other escaped porters had similar stories to tell. But later, when I spoke with a number of captured SLORC soldiers, they either denied the porters' accounts or blamed their officers, who "forced us to behave this way."

I was able to interview one of those officers when, several nights later, a SLORC corporal with ten years' active service was captured. He was extremely thin, would not respond to my questions about torture and rape, and regarded me impassively as I pressed him. "Why," I asked, "are you willing to kill your own people?"

He looked at me intensely. "Because if we don't follow orders we are shot on the spot. This I know. I've seen it happen a number of times. Once in the military we become prisoners in our own army. All of us hate the SLORC leaders, especially Khin Nyunt. They demand that we kill, torture and burn villages."

"Nevertheless," I said, "you're still willing to kill your own people. Why are you exterminating your people's right to freedom and democracy? Don't you know that the whole world has condemned your SLORC leaders?"

"I know nothing," he said, staring into the small fire between us. "If I don't fight, I'm dead."

After ten days of living with the democratic forces, my main concern was to return to the United States with a clear understanding of what they needed and how the western world could help. The next morning I met with David Tharckabaw, the eloquent general secretary of the Overseas Karen Organization, a refugee organization based in Thailand.

He planted himself heavily on a crude wooden bench and spent two hours bringing me up to date on the details of Burma's plight. "Ne Win, Saw

Maung and Khin Nyunt have no sense of morality," he said in his low monotone.

They've injected their 280,000 SLORC soldiers with racist and distorted ideals, with the aim to have their killing machine exterminate our race—not just the Karens, but other ethnic minorities as well: the Shans, Mons, the Rohingyas, Kachins, Karennis and others. SLORC's policy is one of mass slaughter.

The SLORC troops storm into our villages and burn them to the ground—hundreds of them all over the country. They kill our livestock, cut down our fruit trees, burn our crops and food supplies. This is why hundreds of thousands of terrorized refugees are fleeing the country.

Even more tragic is the fact that four or five million others are trapped inside Burma. Either they've been displaced, herded into military secured encampments or have fled to a deplorable existence in dense jungles and mountainous areas all over the country. Many others are too scared to cross the border into Thailand because of the Thai government's support of SLORC and their oppressive policy toward Burmese refugees.

Fixing his eyes on mine, he said, "You ask how the international community can help us. Someone needs to intervene and stop this madness. *Now.*"

Later that same afternoon I was able to speak with U Win Khet, an elderly gentleman and well-known Burmese novelist. He's one of Aung San Suu Kyi's closest colleagues and a cofounder of the National League for Democracy.

Two days after Aung San Suu Kyi's arrest on July 20, 1989, SLORC soldiers surrounded U Win

Khet's residence in Rangoon. But he'd been tipped off beforehand and fled to Manerplaw. That was 16 months ago. Now he was suffering from severe malaria. I met him in a small wooden hut that was serving as the current NLD headquarters.

"What does the future hold for Burma?" I asked, realizing the broad sweep and speculative nature of the question.

Clearly in pain from the malaria, U Win Khet replied weakly: "This struggle is between a handful of military men and the entire population of Burma—people who are literally starving for freedom. We feel the people will win in the end. We will not let go of our democratic aspirations. We will never obey SLORC's demands. We know they'll ruthlessly suppress us. This they have made perfectly clear. But that's their great mistake.

"Now all the democratic forces are standing and fighting against SLORC under one banner. We are united in our struggle for democracy. SLORC's concept is *might is right.* But this concept never wins in the long run. Our conviction is *right is might.*"

Our conversation was interrupted as a piercing mechanical scream filled the air. U Win Khet's attendant raced into the hut. "SLORC jets!" he yelled. He picked U Win Khet up from his bed and carried him to a nearby bomb shelter, where we waited out the attack.

The shelter was a deep ditch protected by heavy logs. Inside with me were half a dozen people—four NLD officials, a young Burmese woman and her two young daughters, who clung to their mother and cried. No one spoke.

After half an hour the Chinese-made F-6 jet fighters tore away and I walked, my legs still trembling, back to NLD headquarters. When U Win Khet returned, my questions had a fresh urgency. "What can the world community do to help you and Burma's democratic movement?"

"All nations should put into immediate effect international trade sanctions and a complete arms embargo," he said. He was shaken by the jet attack and sweating—a symptom of advanced malaria.

"Companies should not invest in Burma, and all other companies that do should divest their interests. Their dollars go toward the further killing of our people. SLORC has no right to the UN seat they've arbitrarily stolen from the people. It should be vacated at once. We also need humanitarian aid to assist the tens of thousands of refugees. These

*Child crying at the entrance to a bomb shelter in Manerplaw*

people are suffering from malnutrition, disease and abuse by the military."

While I was taking his photograph, the jets reappeared. Again, U Win Khet was rushed into a bomb shelter.

That night, a rainstorm swept through the area. Rain in February—midway through the dry season—is unheard of, and seemed an act of divine intervention (since it holds off the bombers). At dawn we managed to get a boat and headed upriver to escape an almost certain air attack on Manerplaw. The sound of rocket and mortar bombing continued without break. After a few hours we climbed ashore and began the five-hour trek over the mountains back to the road and to safety.

As I expected, Manerplaw was severely strafed by SLORC jets the day after we left. There were few deaths; by that time, fortunately, the settlement had been almost totally evacuated.

On March 22, Sleeping Dog Mountain, one of the highest points in the vicinity of Manerplaw, was taken by SLORC soldiers. By March 28, Manerplaw was repeatedly shelled by heavy weapons. The democratic forces withstood the attack and defended their position. Meanwhile, thousands of refugees continued to pour into Thailand, Bangladesh, Laos and China.

For those of us who live in free countries, it's almost impossible to conceive of SLORC's endless atrocities. Most of us have never even seen a single murder victim—how can we fathom impending genocide?

The awarding of the Nobel Peace Prize to Daw Aung San Suu Kyi was a plea for SLORC to abandon its tactics of terror and to free Aung San Suu Kyi and all of Burma's political prisoners. It was a call for the immediate halting of forced relocations, unlawful arrests, mass torture, summary executions and the systematic extermination of ethnic nationalities.

On December 9th, 1991, a group of nine Nobel laureates—including Bishop Desmond Tutu, the Dalai Lama, Dr. Elie Wiesel and Dr. Oscar Arias—drafted and signed a letter to the leaders of SLORC, which read in part:

> We are writing to voice our concern for our fellow Nobelist, Aung San Suu Kyi, and for the people of your country. As the lack of human rights and democracy in your country has caused much suffering and distress, we urge you to enter into dialogue with those leaders you have detained, and so take a step in bringing peace to your troubled country.
>
> By opening up your country to free political debate...you would not only advance the cause of peace, but you would be holding to the honorable Buddhist qualities of humility, understanding, compassion and tolerance.

Needless to say, these sentiments fell on deaf ears.

# *Epilogue*

In the spring of 1992, Burma began to reappear in the news as SLORC announced a series of political changes and "reforms." These were transparent ploys designed to relieve international pressure and improve Burma's abominable reputation on the global scene.

First, SLORC General Saw Maung resigned after a nervous breakdown. Some analysts hypothesize that he was dumped, possibly as a scapegoat for four years of terror. The move apparently was engineered by ambitious SLORC Major General Khin Nyunt, Burma's notorious "Prince of Evil," who experts believe covets the top post. To avoid inflaming an already seething nation, Saw Maung was replaced by SLORC General Than Shwe *(tahn SHWAY)*. Like his former boss, Than Shwe was directly involved in the massacres that took place during the summer of 1988.

While this shakeup occurred, Ne Win—who has not appeared in public for years—ordered all pictures of himself to be removed from public places. What he hoped to gain from such a move remains unclear; but one Burmese resident, quoted in the *San Francisco Chronicle*, suggested that he may be trying to avoid divine retribution. "He wants to try to clean things up," the observer said, "before he passes into the next life as a cockroach."

Regardless of such gestures, though, it's believed that Ne Win remains firmly in power—maneuvering his puppets, from behind the scenes.

On April 28, after a four-month-long "scorched earth" war against the ethnic minorities, SLORC announced over state-controlled media that "the [offensive] has been suspended in view of national unity and goodwill." In fact, SLORC's front line positions were simply digging in for the rainy season, as they do every year. The rains continued through October. September had witnessed the arrival of fresh troops and weapons in preparation for a "final" onslaught against the democratic forces. The rest of Burma enjoyed no seasonal respite from SLORC terror; in Rangoon, Mandalay and the major cities, it was business as usual.

On a more positive note, the Norwegian Government has demonstrated unprecedented support by donating a one hour per day radio program to the democratic opposition, which is being short-wave broadcast directly into Burma. SLORC has tried numerous times to jam the transmission, but it is managing to get through, albeit faintly.

A renewed attempt to force Suu Kyi into exile was made in early May 1992. SLORC authorities allowed Michael Aris, Suu Kyi's husband, to visit her for the first time in over two years. Upon his return from Rangoon, Aris reported that "the offer was repeatedly made to release her if she went into exile."

He went on to say that "[Suu Kyi] never even discussed the matter because she says it is not negotiable....Since the day she began her endeavors, she resolved to stay and see it all through, come what may....In the nearly two and a half years since I last saw Suu, things have not been easy for her, but in the days we spent together she repeatedly pointed out to me that others have suffered much more than she has."

A surprising event occurred on May 15, 1992, when Suu Kyi's 19-year-old son Alexander delivered a speech written by his mother. Transmitted with the permission of the SLORC authorities, this was the first statement the world has received from Suu Kyi since her arrest in July, 1989. Among other things, she wrote:

> The world is watching Burma to see whether the rights of citizens to participate fully in the political process of their country will be conceded; whether the will of the people as expressed through free and fair elections will truly be respected; and whether there will be serious moves to protect human rights by promoting the rule of law and by establishing an independent judiciary.

For the forty million people of Burma, the nightmare continues. Will their long night end, or will the Golden Land become Southeast Asia's next killing fields?

# *How you can help*

In March 1991, Alan Cranston and ten other US Senators submitted a resolution to President Bush urging that the United States begin economic sanctions against Burma's government. Since then, the US has condemned human rights abuses in Burma with tersely worded official statements, has cut off $16 million dollars in aid and has also banned the importation of textiles from Burma.

But a much greater, grassroots movement is necessary to avert full-scale genocide in Burma. Here are some ways that you, personally, can participate in Burma's continuing struggle for democracy:

1. Boycott all businesses that do business in Burma. They include: Amoco, 501 Westlake Park Blvd, Houston TX 77079; PepsiCo, Anderson Hill Road, Purchase NY 10577; Unocal, 1201 West 5th Street, Los Angeles CA 90061.

2. Dean Hardwoods, Box 1595, Wilmington NC 28402 imports teak from Burma. When in doubt, *do not buy teak products!*

3. Write The President, UN Security Council, United Nations, New York NY 10017 and request that the Security Council pass a resolution imposing an international arms embargo on Myanmar (Burma). Enclose a copy to the Secretary General of the United Nations at the same address.

4. Write your elected representatives at one or all of the following addresses, asking them to support economic sanctions and an international arms embargo against the government of Myanmar: The United States House of Representatives, Washington

DC 20515; United States Senate, Washington DC 20510; The President, The White House, Washington DC 20500; The Secretary of State, Washington DC 20520.

5. Write to SLORC and request the unconditional release of Daw Aung San Suu Kyi and U Tin Oo, and the immediate transfer of government to the representatives elected in May 1990. Letters should be addressed to General Than Shwe, Chairman, SLORC, Ministry of Defense, Rangoon, Myanmar.

6. Amnesty International is working tirelessly to improve the human rights situation in Burma and can help you become involved. Write Amnesty International Campaign Office, Burma Section, Suite 406, 655 Sutter St, San Francisco CA 94102. Or call them at 415 441 2114.

7. Boycott tourism in Burma. Tourist dollars don't help the Burmese people—they contribute to their oppression.

8. Become more informed about Burma. Take a look at the materials listed in the *Recommended reading* and *Notes* which follow this section. Here are some useful newsletters: *Burma Alert* , RR 4, Shawville, JOX 270 Quebec, Canada; *Burma Review,* Box 7726, Rego Park NY 11374; *B.U.R.M.A.,* Box 1076, Silom Post Office, Bangkok 10505 Thailand.

9. Support the Burma Project USA. Directed by Alan Clements, the author of this book, the Burma Project is a human rights organization dedicated to increasing international awareness about the crisis in Burma. Founded in January 1991, it's waged an extensive public education campaign that has included interviews and photographs in *Newsweek,* an interview by ABC television for *Nightline,* lectures at

Amnesty International events and programs on Voice of America radio.

The Burma Project also conducts investigative trips inside Burma to monitor human rights abuses, submitting documentation to the United Nations as well as to media sources. It arranged the 1991 California visit of Prime Minister Sein Win of Burma's exiled democratic government. Dr. Win fully endorses the work of the Burma Project and has requested that the organization serve as Northern California contact for his government-in-exile.

The Burma Project USA is a nonprofit, tax-exempt organization that depends on individual donations and foundation grants. Your support will be greatly appreciated. To send a contribution or to request information, please write to the Burma Project USA, 45 Oak Road, Larkspur CA 94939 (415 924 6447; fax: 415 924 6101).

# *Recommended reading*

Aung San Suu Kyi. *Freedom From Fear and Other Writings*. Penguin, 1991.

Lintner, Bertil. *Outrage*. White Lotus Publishing Co (16, Soi 47, Sukhumvit, Box 1141, Bangkok Thailand), 1991.

Silverstein, Josef. *Military Rule and the Politics of Stagnation*. Cornell University Press, 1977.

Smith, Martin. *Burma: Insurgency and the Politics of Ethnicity*. Zed Books, 1991.

Staud, Ervin. *The Roots of Evil*. Cambridge University Press, 1991.

# *Notes*

*Sources for the facts in this book are listed below by page numbers and brief subject descriptions. Full publication and/or contact data is given the first time a work or organization is cited. If it's mentioned in the **Recommended Reading** or **How You Can Help** sections above, it's bolded when first cited, which indicates that the publication and/or contact information is in those sections.*

11. Killing health workers. Physicians for Human Rights (100 Boyleston St., Suite 702, Boston MA 02116), November 1991.

15–19. Burma's history. **Lintner**, 14-36; **Silverstein**, 3-31, 54-79; David Steinberg. *Burma: A Socialist Nation of Southeast Asia.* Westview Press, 1982, 1-72.

20. Atrocities against monks. "Bullets in Alms Bowls," *Time,* November 19, 1990.

23–25. Ne Win's rule. Lintner, 37-86; Silverstein, 80-166; Steinberg, 73-93.

25. Bloodbath casualties. *Nightline* (ABC TV), November 29, 1991.

25–26. New optimism. Lintner, 113-120.

26–27. SLORC takes over. Lintner, 131-135.

27–28. Elections announced. International Human Rights Law Group (1601 Connecticut Avenue NW, Suite 700, Washington DC 20009), May 19, 1990.

28–29. Suu Kyi's background. Philip Kreager, "Aung San Suu Kyi and the Peaceful Struggle for Human Rights in Burma" in **Aung San Suu Kyi**, 291.

29–30. Suu Kyi's campaign. Aung San Suu Kyi, 198-204; Kreager, 297-317.

30. Draconian restrictions. *State of Fear.* Article XIX (90 Borough High Street, London SE1 1LL UK), 1991.

31. Suu Kyi challenges SLORC. *B.U.R.M.A.* , October 1991.

31. Suu Kyi's letter. Aung San Suu Kyi, 220.

31. Suu Kyi's bravery. Kreager, 305-306.

32. Suu Kyi defends armed forces. Kreager, 305.

32–33. Mass Relocation. "Burma: 'Horror Story' of Mass Relocations," *New York Times,* March 20, 1990.

33. New town conditions. *B.U.R.M.A.,* August 1990.

33. Martyr's Day demonstrations. "A Rich Country Gone Wrong," *New Yorker,* Oct 9, 1989.

33. Avoiding a "killing field"; Suu Kyi arrested for "endangering the state." **Amnesty International** *Briefing,* September 1990.

34-35. Suu Kyi demands transfer; hunger strike. Kreager, 317.

35. Election results. Josef Silverstein, "Burma's Woman of Destiny" in Aung Son Suu Kyi, 276.

35. Nuremberg-type trials. "Burmese Generals Fear 'Nuremberg-type trials,'" *The Nation* (Bangkok newspaper), December 7, 1989.

35. NLD supporters imprisoned. Kreager, 316.

35. Political prisoners. *Asia Watch* (485 Fifth Avenue, New York NY 10017), August 1990.

35-36. Torture centers and methods. Amnesty International *Report,* October 1990.

32-36. Legal oppression under SLORC. Lawyers Committee for Human Rights *Report* (10th Floor, 330 Seventh Ave., New York, NY 10001), April 1991.

51. Attacks on monasteries. **Kolvig,** 45-47; "Bullets in Alms Bowls," *Time,* November 19, 1990.

52. Fear corrupts. Aung San Suu Kyi, 180.

55-56. Student repatriations. Amnesty International *Briefing,* September 1990; US Committee for Refugees *Report* (1025 Vermont Avenue NW, Suite 920, Washington DC 20005), May 1990.

58-59. Chaungsone story. Also see *B.U.R.M.A.,* October 1991.

59. Deforestation. United Nations World Development *Report,* July 1991, Vol. 4, No. 4; *Financial Times* (London), June 1990.

60. Moynihan's address to Congress. US Committee for Refugees *Report,* May 1990.

60. Oil companies. Lintner, 178.

60. US multi-nationals. *B.U.R.M.A.,* October 1991.

60-61. Van Kloberg. "For Van Kloberg, Burmese Regime is Yet Another Unpopular Client," *Lobby Talk,* November 1991; "Magazines' Ruse Tests the Ethics of D.C. Lobbyists," *San Francisco Chronicle,* December 28, 1991.

61. The heroin trade. "Field of Dreams," *Far Eastern Economic Review,* February 20, 1992; Kolvig, 25-26; interview with Bertil Lintner, **Burma Project USA.**

61. Chinese arms swapped for Burmese heroin. *United States Congressional Record—Senate,* April 7, 1992.

62. China arms shipments to Burma. "3 Senators Asking Action," *New York Times,* April 1992; "Oiling the Iron Fist," *Far Eastern Economic Review,* December 6, 1990.

62. Chemical weapons. "Big Oil and the Burmese Military," *Washington Post,* May 29, 1991.

62. Brothels. UNICEF *Report on Myanmar,* March 16, 1992.

62. HIV-positive prostitutes. "Burmese Girls with HIV 'Put to Death,'" *The Australian,* April 6, 1992.

62. Thousands of prostitutes injected. "Topple Burma junta: Aust. urged to stop support." *The Courier Mail,* June 18, 1992.

71. Nobel Peace Prize. Aung San Suu Kyi, 236-237.

72. Muslims suffocated. "Burma Forces 15,000 Muslims into Human Shield," *The Australian,* January 21, 1992.

72. Mosque murders. "Burmese Massacred Muslims at Prayer," *The Australian,* April 9. 1992.

72. Muslim women raped. *B.U.R.M.A.,* April 1992.

72. Refugees. **Burma Review**, January 1992.

74. Porters. David Tharckabaw interview, Burma Project USA; Aung San Suu Kyi, 215-216.

75. Carl Gustav rockets. Lintner, 140.

75–76. Porters interview. Burma Project USA.

77. SLORC corporal interview. Burma Project USA.

77–78. David Tharckabaw interview. Burma Project USA.

78–81. U Win Khet interview. Burma Project USA.

82. Nobel laureates' letter. Oslo, December 9, 1991.

83. SLORC leader retires. "Saw Maung Resigns," *Bangkok Post,* April 24, 1992.

83. Khin Nuynt called "Prince of Evil." "The Prince of Evil Spreads Fear and Loathing," *Bangkok Post,* May 27, 1991.

83. Than Shwe's appointment. "Burma's Long Road to Freedom," *Bangkok Post,* May 11, 1992.

83–84. Ne Win's fears; offensive halted. "Ne Win Urges End to Displays of his Pictures," *Bangkok Post,* May 6, 1992; "Burma Calls Off Attack on Leading Rebel Force," *San Francisco Chronicle,* April 29, 1992.

84. Suu Kyi remains detained. "Husband Finds Burmese Dissident Still 'Indomitable,'" *New York Times,* May 18, 1992.

85. Suu Kyi's statement. *International Human Rights Law Group,* May 14, 1992.

86. Cranston address. Congressional Record, March 12, 1991.

# *Index*

ABSDF, *see* All Burma Students' Democratic Front

ABYMU, *see* All Burma Young Monks' Union

acknowledgments, 6-7

AIDS, 62

All Burma Students' Democratic Front (ABSDF), 54-54; *also see* democratic forces

All Burma Young Monks' Union (ABYMU), 49-50; *also see* democratic forces

Aloka, 49-50

Amnesty International, 35, 56, 87-88

Amoco, 60, 86

Arakanese, 9, 15

Arias, Oscar, 82

Aris, Alexander, 85

Aris, Michael, 29, 84

Aung San
assassinated, 18
daughter of, 28
independence leader, 16-18
pictured, 17, 28

Aung San Suu Kyi
arrest of, 33-34, 52
book by, 52, 88
background of, 28-30
demand release of, 87
"grace under pressure," 6
hunger strike by, 34-35
inspiring leadership of, 52, 57
Nobel Peace Prize, 71, 82
offered release/exile, 84
pictured, 7, 28, 29, 34
praised by Dalai Lama, 4
pronunciation of name, 28
"Revolution of the Spirit" campaign, 30-32
Shwedagon pagoda speech, 29-30
on SLORC tactics, 31
speech delivered by son, 85

*The Australian,* 62

Bangkok, 21-23, 53

Bangladesh, 8-9

BBC, 47

BHP, 60

BIA, *see* Burmese Independent Army

Bo Mya, General, 69

boycotts recommended, 86-87

Brang Seng, 69

Bryson, John, 36-38

BSPP, *see* Burmese Socialist Program Party

Buddhism
Burmese followers of, 9
monasticism of, 13
spiritual banishment from, 51
teachings of, 12, 14

Buddhist monks
atrocities against, 20, 47, 49-50
influence of sanga, 50-51
SLORC kills Chaungsone monk, 58-59
SLORC puppets replace, 51

Burma
Caretaker Government of, 19
colonization of, 15-16
coup by SLORC, 26
deforestation of, 59
democratic forces in jungle, 54
destruction of educated in, 27, 48
drug trade, 61
during World War II, 17-18
economic decline of, 24-25
ethnic minorities of, 9, 15-16
government-in-exile, 68
granted independence, 18
maps of, 8-9
nationwide strikes, 25-26
need for international support, 80
political parties of, 23-24
population of, 8-9
renamed Myanmar, 38
school closings, 48
SLORC-controlled media, 44-45
Thai sex industry and, 62
tourism to, 87

*Burma Alert,* 87

Burmans, 9, 15

Burma Project USA, 87-88

*Burma Review,* 87

Burma Rights Movement for Action (B.U.R.M.A.), 33, 87

Burmese Embassy in Bangkok, 21-22

Burmese Independent Army (BIA), 17

Burmese resistance, *see* democratic forces
Burmese Socialist Program Party (BSPP), 23-24, 26

Cambodian genocide, 36-38
Caretaker Government, *see* junta
Carl Gustav rocket, 75
Ceausescu, Nicolae, 61
Chaowalit, General, 55-56
Chaungsone, 58
children murdered, 43, 56-58, 69-70
China, 8-9, 61-62
Chins, 9
Christianity, 16
citations, 89-91
Clements, Alan
    becomes Buddhist monk, 12-13
    visits Rangoon, 39-52
    visits jungle, 53-59, 63-70, 72-81
Dalai Lama
    foreword by, 4-5
    letter by, 82
Daw Aung San Suu Kyi, *see* Aung San Suu Kyi
Dean Hardwoods, 86
deforestation, 59
democratic forces,
    aspirations of, 56-57
    headquarter conditions of, 64
    *Also see* All Burma Students' Democratic Front (ABSDF); All Burma Young Monks' Union (ABYMU); Burma Rights Movement for Action (B.U.R.M.A.); Kachin Independence Organization (KIO); Karen National Union (KNU); National Coalition Government of the Union of Burma (NCGUB); National League for Democracy (NLD); students
drug trade, 61
Duke, David, 61

endnotes, 89-91
enslaved porters, 74-76
ethnic minorities, 9, 15-16

*Far Eastern Economic Review*, 61
foreword, 4-5

filmmaker, interview with, 42-44
*Freedom from Fear*, 52, 88

Gandhi, Mahatma, 4
genocide
    Burma as next, 38, 81
    Cambodian, 36-38
"Golden Land," *see* Burma
Great Britain, 15-16
Gyi, U, 45-46

"helicopter" torture, 36
heroin trade, 61
how you can help, 86-88
Hussein, Saddam, 61

"ice treatment" torture, 36
India, 8-9, 16
inflation, 24-25, 39
Insein Prison, 34
"iron road" torture, 36

Japan, 17-18
junta
    Caretaker Government of, 19
    changes by ruling, 23-24
    election defeat of, 35
    financing of, 60
    *Also see* SLORC

Kachin Independence Organization (KIO), 69
Kachins, 9, 15-16, 72
Kampuchea, 38
Karen National Union (KNU), 54, 69
Karenni, 9, 15
Karens
    civil war by, 18-19
    ethnic minority, 15-16
    flee SLORC troops, 72
    shown on map, 9
Khin Nyunt, Major General
    ambitions of, 83-84
    announces Manerplaw offensive, 71
    character of, 78
    hated by SLORC soldiers, 77
    media propaganda, 44, 46, 51
    pictured, 26
    pronunciation of name, 44
Khmer Rouge, 38

killing fields
    Burma as next, 38, 81
    Cambodian, 36-38
King, Martin Luther, 4
Ko, 11-12, 19, 25
Kolvig, Eric, 88

Land of 10,000 Pagodas, *see* Burma
Laos, 8-9
*Life,* 36-37
Lintner, Bertil, 61, 88
love story, 65-68

Mae Pah ridge line, 73-74
Mahasi Sayadaw, 13
malaria, 22, 27, 64, 69, 79
Mandalay, 9, 49, 51
Manerplaw
    ABSDF headquarters, 54
    arrival in, 64
    bombing of, 79-81
    described after offensive, 73
    Sein Win arrives in, 68
    shown on map, 9
    SLORC offensive against, 71-75
Manglapus, Raul, 35
Manipur, 72
maps, 8-9
Martyrs' Day, 33
media
    lack of outside, 47
    SLORC-controlled, 44-45, 51
Mizoram, 72
Moei River, 54, 63
Mons, 9, 15, 72
Moynihan, Daniel, 60
Muslims, 72
Myanmar, 38; *also see* Burma

Naga Hills tribespeople, 72
Naing Aung, Dr., 55
National Coalition Government of
    the Union of Burma (NCGUB),
    68-69
National League for Democracy
    (NLD)
    election victories by, 35
    objective of, 28
    Suu Kyi campaigns for, 30
    U Win Khet cofounder of, 78
NCGUB, see National Coalition Gov-
    ernment of the Union of Burma

Ne Win, General
    avoiding divine retribution, 83
    Caretaker Government of, 19,
        23-24
    changes name, 19
    character of, 77-78
    imprisons U Tin Oo, 13
    pronunciation of name, 19
    renames Burma, 38
    responds to demonstrations, 25
    *Also see* SLORC
*Newsweek,* 48, 87
"new towns," 33, 47; *also see*
    relocation camps
*New Yorker,* 33
*New York Times,* 32-33
*Nightline,* 25, 87
NLD, *see* National League for
    Democracy
Nobel laureates, 82
Nobel Peace Prize, 71, 82
notes, 89-91
Nu, U, 18-19

opium, 61
Overseas Karen Organization, 77

PepsiCo, 86
Petro-Canada, 60
pilgrim's visa, 13
Pol Pot, 38
population of Burma, 8-9
porters, enslaved, 74-76
"Prince of Evil," *see* Khin Nyunt
propaganda, 41, 44-45, 48, 51
prostitutes murdered, 62

rainforests, rape of, 59
Rangoon
    "beautification" campaign, 41
    changed character of, 39-44
    impact of colonization on, 16
    massacre in, 11-12
    population of, 9
    shown on map, 9
Rangoon General Hospital, 11
Rangoon University, 16
recommended reading, 87, 88
refugees, 72
    flee Manerplaw offensive, 81
    flee to Thailand, 38, 55-56, 72
    Overseas Karen Org., 77

relocation camps, 32-33, 38; *also see* "new towns"
"Revolution of the Spirit" campaign, 30, 52
   *Also see* Aung San Suu Kyi
Rohingyas, 9, 72

Salween River, 73
*San Francisco Chronicle*, 83
sanga, 50-51
Saw Maung, General
   character of, 77-78
   head of SLORC, 26
   media propaganda of, 44, 51
   pictured, 26
   resignation of, 83
secret police, *see* SLORC
Sein Win, Dr., 68-69, 73, 88
Shans, 9, 15, 18-19
Shwedagon pagoda, 48-49
   Suu Kyi speech at, 29-30
Silverstein, Josef, 88
Sleeping Dog Mountain, 81
SLORC
   announced reforms by, 83-84
   announces free elections, 27-28
   arms sales to, 62
   arrests Suu Kyi, 33
   attacks against educated, 27, 48
   attacks against monks, 20, 49-51
   "beautification" campaign, 41
   campaign restrictions by, 30-32
   children murdered by,
      43, 56-58, 69-70
   coup by, 26-27
   destroying environment, 59
   enslaving porters, 74-76
   fails to transfer power, 35
   forced relocation by, 32-33
   Manerplaw offensive by, 71-75
   massacres by, 11-12, 56-58, 71-72
   Nobel laureates letter to, 82
   parallels with Khmer Rouge, 38
   pronunciation of name, 26
   propaganda, 41, 44-45, 48, 51
   role in opium trade, 61
   soldiers described, 39
   synonym for terror, 23
   terror tactics, 45-46, 58, 78, 84
   tortures used by, 36, 74
   US corporate complicity with,
      60–61

village destroyed by, 46-47
Western joint investments, 60-61
*Also see* Khin Nyunt; Ne Win; Saw Maung; Than Shwe
Smith, Martin, 88
sources, 89-91
State Law and Order Restoration Council, *see* SLORC
Staud, Ervin, 88
students
   attacks on, 27, 48, 54-55
   hiding in Thailand, 55-56
   infected with malaria, 64
   relates sister and brother's deaths, 56-58
   *Also see* democratic forces
Suu Kyi, *see* Aung San Suu Kyi
Swedish rocket, 75

taxi driver, interview with, 47-48
"teak barns," 59
Thailand
   Burmese refugees flee to, 72
   escape to, 38
   sex industry of, 62
   shown on map, 8-9
   students hiding in, 55-56
   "teak barns" and Thai military, 59
thakins, 16-17
Than Shwe, General, 26, 83, 87
Tharchabaw, David, 77
Thirty Comrades, 17
*Time*, 20, 48
Tin Oo, U, 13-14, 34, 87
torture, 36, 74
Tutu, Bishop Desmond, 82

U, *honorific title; see the name without the U*
UNICEF, 62
UN Development Programme, 59
Unocal, 60, 86

Van Kloberg Associates, 60-61
*Voice of America*, 47

"walking the seashore" torture, 36
"wet submarine" torture, 36
what you can do, 86-88
Wiesel, Elie, 82
Win Khet, U, 78-81
World War II, 17-18, 61

*The Real Story series
is based on a simple idea—
political books don't have to be boring.
Short, well-written and to the point,
Real Story books are meant to be <u>read</u>.*

*If you liked this book, check out some of
the others in the Real Story series:*

### The Decline and Fall of the American Empire
### Gore Vidal

Vidal is one of our most important—and wittiest—social critics. This little book is the perfect intro-duction to his political thought        *Fall, 1992*

### What Uncle Sam Really Wants
### Noam Chomsky

A brilliant analysis of the real motivations behind US foreign policy, from one of America's most popular speakers. Full of astounding information.
                                                            *Fall, 1992*

### Who Killed JFK?            Carl Oglesby

This brief but fact-filled book gives you the inside story on the most famous crime of this century. You won't be able to put it down.        *Spring, 1992*

Real Story books are available at most good book-stores, or send $5 per book + $2 shipping *per order* (not per book) to Odonian Press, Box 7776, Berkeley CA 94707. Please write for information on quantity discounts, or call us at 510 524 3143.